LHBEC

ENVIRONMENTALLY SUSTAINABLE ECONOMIC DEVELOPMENT: BUILDING ON BRUNDTLAND

UNESCO

The authors are responsible for the choice and the presentation
of the facts contained in this book and for the opinions expressed therein, which are
not necessarily those of UNESCO and do not commit the Organization.

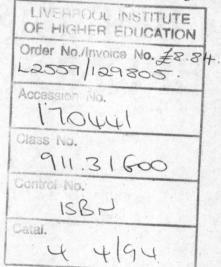

Graphic design: Ursula Wöss
Computer-assisted layout: Astera Koskas

First published in 1991 by the United Nations Educational,
Scientific and Cultural Organization
7 Place de Fontenoy, 75700 Paris
Printed by Imprimerie Bietlot, Gilly

Second impression 1992

ISBN 92-3-102781-6

Foreword

Highlighting the value of our 'natural capital', this book makes it clear that unless development is distinguished from economic growth, the turn-off towards sustainable development will be missed. It indicates that too many warning signs have already been ignored suggesting that, in North and South alike, we are moving in the wrong direction and that there may be few, if any, short-cuts back.

Situated at the crossroads of culture, science, communication and education, UNESCO has long been a proponent of the interdisciplinary approach recommended by the World Commission on Environment and Development. There is no doubt that such an approach, further elaborated here, is necessary to deal with the complex problems of environment and development.

This publication has been produced to reinforce the concept of ecological economics as the world prepares for the 1992 United Nations Conference on Environment and Development to be held in Brazil. By focusing on key issues that need to be further explored in order to achieve a more equitable and environmentally sustainable economy, I am confident that it will make a valuable contribution to this essential objective.

Federico Mayor
Director–General,
United Nations
Educational, Scientific and
Cultural Organization

Contents

Preface

We are delighted to have been invited to preface this book for four reasons. First, because it sets a realistic and fair stage for the important UNCED 1992 conference. Second, because it acknowledges much more development is needed in the South. Third, because that needed development and growth must be accommodated by the North. Fourth, burdensharing or reparation for the North's historic overuse of global environmental functions — both as source of natural resources and sink for wastes — is firmly accepted by the almost entirely Northern authors. This is refreshing.

We have not been too encouraged by the North's reaction to the Brundtland report over the four years since its publication. Therefore, we warmly endorse the clear thinking expressed in this book. The fact that two Nobel laureate economists are among the authors (Haavelmo and Tinbergen) raises our hopes that economists will put sustainability higher on their agendas for serious work in the 1990s. We fully share the authors' view that the transition is urgent and we find their suggestions on how to achieve it to be sensible. Now the difficult part, mustering the political will, is up to us and our UNCED '92 colleagues.

The Honourable Emil Salim
Minister of State
Environment and Population
Jakarta, Indonesia

The Honourable Jose Lutzenberger
Secretary of State
for Environment
Brasilia D.F., Brazil

Introduction

Right at the outset, we want to acknowledge our major debt to the Brundtland
Commission's 1987 report, *Our Common
Future*. In particular, we greatly admire
the achievement of the World Commission on Environment and Development
(WCED) in garnering political consensus
on the need for sustainable development.
We use this report as our springboard,
though we are far less comprehensive.
Of the four elements of environmental
sustainability (poverty, population,
technology, and life–style) we focus on
only life–style, technology and population, with that order of emphasis reflecting our skills. Poverty is only dealt with
through our suggestions for a more
equitable international income distribution. We acknowledge, however, that
poverty as well as debt are for some
countries more pressing concerns than
the environment.

Our aim is to follow Brundtland's
lead on the need for a rapid transition to
sustainability. We bolster Brundtland's
case for the transition, because we feel
that the need for this transition is not yet
adequately recognized. We then go on to
suggest specifics of what is needed to
achieve the transition. We leave to
others the more important task, namely
how to implement the transition and how
to muster the political will for changes
that will be painful, but essential. We feel
that understanding the necessity and
general direction of the transition is a
precondition for mustering the political
will.

All authors have read and discussed
each other's chapters and have reached
consensus that the contributions included in this volume are not only
compatible with each other, but also
mutually reinforcing. We collaborated,
first, because we felt that we were all
already thinking along similar lines,
judging from our previous writings, and,
second, because we all feel strongly that
the next step for the transition to
sustainability is agreement on the
implications of what Brundtland advocated. We have deliberately retained a
certain overlap between some chapters
in an effort to stress the notion that,
irrespective of the direction from which
the subject is approached, the same
conclusion is reached.

The conclusion is that economic

activity cannot proceed any longer under the banner of 'business as usual'. Specifically it is no longer tenable to make economic growth, as conventionally perceived and measured, the unquestioned objective of economic development policy. The old concept of growth, which we designate 'throughput growth', with its reliance on an ever–increasing throughput of energy and other natural materials, cannot be sustained, and must yield to an imaginative pursuit of economic ends that are less resource intensive. The way we undervalue natural capital services and fail to account for natural asset degradation often means that we are impoverishing ourselves while imagining that our economies are growing. The new approach requires a concerted effort at remoulding consumer's preferences, and steering wants in the direction of environmentally benign activities, while simultaneously reducing throughput per unit of final product, including services.

Earlier studies of environmental limits to growth emphasized the source limits (depletion of petroleum, copper, etc.). Experience has shown, however, that the sink constraints (greenhouse, ozone depletion, local air and water pollution, etc.) are the more stringent. Because sink functions are common property to a greater extent than source functions, this overuse is less correctable by the automatic market adjustment.

Acceleration of technological development is therefore required to reduce the natural resource content of given economic activities. We feel this important acceleration can be achieved in a way that will satisfy both optimists and pessimists. We suggest substantially increased taxes on throughput (such as carbon emission or mineral severance taxes). This should please the optimists because it will accelerate new technologies. It will please the pessimists because it will reduce environmentally stressful throughput. Since we must tax something in order to raise needed public revenue, why not tax the things we want to reduce (pollution and depletion) rather than the things we want to increase (employment and income)? Because pollution and depletion can never be reduced to zero there is no danger of taxing our source of revenue out of existence, no matter how high the tax rate. As we gain revenue from these environmental taxes we can ease up on income taxes, especially on low incomes, even to the extent of using some of the new revenues to finance a negative income tax on very low incomes. We urgently call for fundamental changes in our economic objectives, as well as in our modes of behaviour. Towards this end, the co–operation of all humankind is necessary.

Brundtland's call for sustainable development has elicited two opposing reactions. One is to revert to a definition of sustainable development as "growth as usual", although at a slower rate. The other reaction is to define sustainable development as "development without growth in throughput beyond environmental carrying capacity". WCED leaders (Brundtland, 1989; McNeill, 1990) seem themselves to be torn between these two directions for operationalizing their concept.

Two realisms conflict. On the one hand, political realism rules out income redistribution and population stability as politically difficult, if not impossible; therefore the world economy has to expand 'by a factor of five or ten' in order to cure poverty. On the other hand, ecological realism accepts that the world economy has already exceeded the sustainable limits of the global ecosystem and that a five-to-tenfold expansion of anything remotely resembling the present economy would simply speed us from today's long run unsustainablity to imminent collapse. We believe that in conflicts between biophysical realities and political realities, the latter must eventually give ground. The planet will transit to sustainability: the choice is between society planning for an orderly transition, or letting physical limits and environmental damage dictate the timing and course of the transition.

While we agree with Brundtland that we should seek to limit, arrest or even reduce the throughput associated with economic activity, we are far less sanguine about our ability to achieve this quickly. The vast expansion in economic activity projected by Brundtland is therefore bound to be associated with major rises in throughput. This does not involve any difference in theory between Brundtland and ourselves; it merely reflects the observable fact that successful substitution of human–made capital for natural resources is slow and limited, and that the necessary technology cannot be organized on cue as the optimists would wish.

Following the dictionary distinction between growth and development, 'to grow' means to increase in size by the assimilation or accretion of materials; 'to develop' means to expand or realize the potentialities of, to bring to a fuller, greater or better state. When something grows it gets quantitatively bigger; when it develops it gets qualitatively better, or at least different. Quantitative growth and qualitative improvement follow different laws. Our planet develops over time without growing. Our economy, a subsystem of the finite and non–growing earth, must eventually adapt to a similar pattern of development without throughput growth. The time for such adaptation is now.

An alternative formulation would be to say that physical inputs must cease growing, but that value of output can continue to increase as long as technological development permits. Of course if physical input is limited, then by the law of conservation of matter–energy, so is physical output. This is equivalent to saying that quantitative growth in throughput is not permitted, but qualitative improvement in services rendered can develop with new technology. In other words we are back to the formulation of development (increasing value of output) without growth (physical throughput constant). Throughput is treated as an aggregate, and clearly some components are more important than others environmentally. For many purposes, energy is the dominant and critical component.

Unfortunately, current GNP accounting conventions conflate growth and development, counting both as "economic growth". We sharply distinguish between throughput growth (growth proper) and efficiency improvement (development in the dictionary sense).

Once these distinctions are accepted it is reasonable to ask: Can development without throughput growth (sustainable development) cure existing poverty? Our belief is that it cannot. Qualitative improvement in the efficiency with which resources are used will greatly help, but will not be sufficient to cure poverty. The reduction of throughput intensity per dollar of GNP in some rich countries is all to the good, but means little to poor countries still striving for adequate food, clothing and shelter. Basic necessities have a large and irreducible physical dimension, unlike say information processing.

The Brundtland proposal to alleviate poverty by an annual 3 per cent global rise in per capita income translates initially into annual per capita income increments of $633 for the United States; $3.6 for Ethiopia; $5.4 for Bangladesh; $7.5 for Nigeria; $10.8 for China and $10.5 for India. By the end of ten years, such growth will have raised Ethiopia's per capita income by $41 (hardly sufficient to dent poverty there) while that of the United States will have risen by $7,257. The greater disparity of international income levels that would result calls into question the desirability of Brundtland's projections.

It is neither ethical nor helpful to the environment to expect poor countries to cut or arrest their development, which tends to be highly associated with throughput growth. Therefore the rich countries, which after all are responsible for most of today's environmental damage, and whose material well–being can sustain a halt to or even a decline in throughput growth, must take the lead in this respect. Poverty reduction will require considerable growth, as well as development, in developing countries. But ecological constraints are real and more growth for the poor must be balanced by negative throughput growth for the rich.

Development by the rich must be used to free resources (source and sink functions of the environment) for growth and development so urgently needed by the poor. Large–scale transfers to the poorer countries also will be required, especially as the impact of economic stability in rich countries may depress terms of trade and lower economic activity in developing countries. Higher prices for the exports of poorer countries therefore will be required. Most importantly, population stability is essential to reduce the need for growth everywhere, but especially where population growth is highest, that is, in the poor countries.

Politically, it is very difficult to face up to the need for income redistribution and population stability. If the concept of sustainable development becomes a verbal formula for glossing over these harsh realities, then it will have been a big step backwards. It is in this sense that we, the authors of this volume, are seeking to build on Brundtland before the tempest of conventional political 'realisms' erodes the foundations that WCED constructed with such care and foresight.

Such an agenda will be exceptionally difficult to implement, and many other issues are involved that are not addressed in this volume, but of which we are acutely aware. Markets, for example, will have to learn to function without expansion, without wars, without wastes and without advertising that encourages waste. Economic policy will have to suppress certain activities in order to allow others to expand, so that the sum total remains within the biophysical budget constraint of a non–growing throughput. This adds up to a formidable political agenda. That is why exceptional political wisdom and leadership are so urgently required. ■

Acknowledgements

We acknowledge the constructive reviews of Vinod Dubey and Herman G. Van der Tak.

References

BRUNDTLAND, G. H. 1989. *Global Change and Our Common Future.* Washington, D.C., Benjamin Franklin Lecture (2 May). *Environment,* Vol. 31, pp. 16–20, 40–43.

McNEILL, J. 1990. Sustainable Development, Economics and the Growth Imperative. Paper presented to the Workshop On the Economics of Sustainable Development, 23–26 January, Washington, D.C., United States Environmental Protection Agency.

WCED, 1987. *Our Common Future* (The Brundtland Report). Oxford, World Commission on Environment and Development/Oxford University Press. 393 pp.

The case that the world has reached limits

More precisely that current throughput growth in the global economy cannot be sustained

Robert Goodland

'It took Britain half the resources of the planet to achieve its prosperity; how many planets will a country like India require?'

Mahatma Gandhi
(when asked if, after independence, India would attain British standards of living)

Introduction

The aim of this chapter is to present the case that limits to growth have already been reached, that further input growth will take the planet further away from sustainability, and that we are rapidly foreclosing options for the future, possibly by overshooting limits (Catton, 1982). This chapter seeks to convince the reader of the urgent need to convert to a sustainable economy, rather than the related and equally or more important need of poverty alleviation. The political will to transit to sustainability will be mustered only when the need for the transition is perceived. The crucial next step — how to muster that political will — is deferred to a subsequent book.

Right at the start, plaudits for Brundtland's heroic achievement: elevating 'sustainability' as a planetary goal now espoused by practically all nations, the United Nations family, and the World Bank. In July 1989, leaders of the Group of Seven major industrialized nations called for 'the early adoption, worldwide, of policies based on sustainable development'. The whole world owes Brundtland an enormous debt for this tremendous feat and we admire her political wisdom. This chapter builds on Brundtland's lead and explores the implications of sustainability. It is assumed as given that the world is being run unsustainably now — being fuelled by inherited fossil fuels is the best single example. Non–renewable oil and gas provide 60 per cent of global energy with barely fifty years of proven reserves.

Brundtland said that meeting essential needs requires 'a new era of economic growth' for nations in which the majority are poor. The report (WCED, 1987) anticipates 'a five– to tenfold increase in world industrial output'. Two years later, this 'sustainable growth' conclusion was reemphasized by the Secretary General of the Brundtland Commission: 'A fivefold to tenfold increase in economic activity would be required over the next 50 years' to achieve sustainability (MacNeill, 1989).

The global ecosystem and the economic subsystem

A single measure — population times per capita resource consumption — encapsulates what is needed to achieve sustainability. This is the scale of the human economic subsystem with respect to that of the global ecosystem on which it depends, and of which it is a part. The global ecosystem is the source of all material inputs feeding the economic subsystem, and is the sink for all its wastes. Population times per capita resource consumption is the total flow — throughput — of resources from the ecosystem to the economic subsystem, then back to the ecosystem as waste, as dramatized in Figure 1. The upper diagram (A) illustrates the bygone era when the economic subsystem was small relative to the size of the global ecosystem. The lower diagram (B) depicts a situation much nearer to today in which the economic subsystem is very large relative to the global ecosystem. Population times per capita resource use is refined by Tinbergen and Hueting (see Chapter 4), and by Ehrlich and Ehrlich (1990).

The global ecosystem's source and sink functions have limited capacity to support the economic subsystem. The imperative, therefore, is to maintain the size of the global economy to within the capacity of the ecosystem to sustain it. Speth (1989) calculates that it took the whole of human history to grow to the $60–billion–dollar–scale economy of 1900. Today, the world economy grows by this amount every two years. Unchecked, today's $20 trillion global economy may be five times bigger only one generation or so hence.

It seems unlikely that the world can sustain a doubling of the economy, let alone Brundtland's five– to ten–fold increase. Throughput growth is not the way to reach sustainability; we cannot 'grow' our way into sustainability. The global ecosystem, which is the source of all the resources needed for the economic subsystem, is finite and has limited regenerative and assimilative capacities. It looks inevitable that the next century will be occupied by double the number of people in the human economy consuming sources and burdening sinks with their wastes.

The global ecosystem is the sink for all the wastes created by the economic subsystem, and this sink has limited assimilative capacity. When the economic subsystem was small relative to the global ecosystem (Fig. 1A), then the sources and sinks were large and limits were irrelevant. Leading thinkers, such as Ehrlich and Ehrlich (1990), Hardin (1991), Boulding (1991), Daly (1990*a*, 1990*b*, 1991*a*, 1991*b*, 1991*c*), as well as the Club of Rome (Meadows et al., 1974), have shown for years that the world is no longer 'empty', the economic subsystem is large relative to the biosphere, and the capacities of the biosphere's sources and sinks are being stressed (Fig. 1B).

Localized limits to global limits

This chapter presents the case that the economic subsystem has reached or exceeded important source and sink limits. There is little doubt that we have already fouled our nest: practically nowhere on this planet are signs of the human economy absent. From the centre of Antarctica to Mount Everest, human wastes are obvious and increasing. It is not possible to find a sample of ocean water without a sign of the 20 billion tonnes of human wastes added annually. PCBs and other persistent toxic chemicals, like DDT and heavy metal

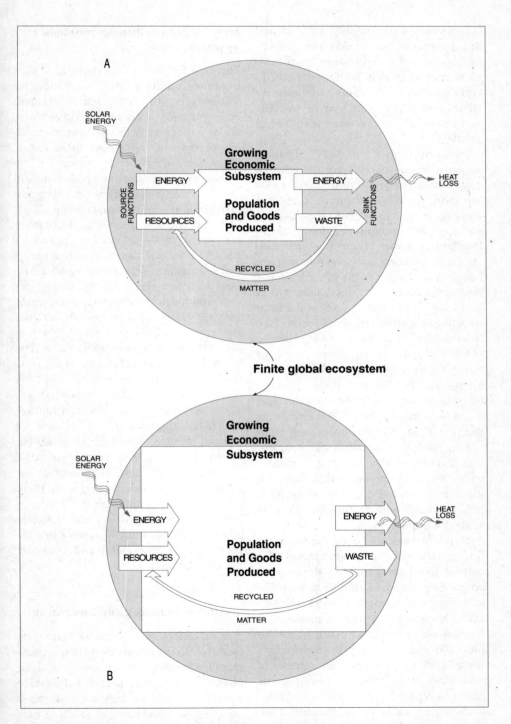

*Figure 1:   The finite global ecosystem relative to the growing economic subsystem
            (after Daly, 1990a; Goodland and Daly, 1990)*

compounds, have already accumulated throughout the marine ecosystem. One–fifth of the world's population breathes air more poisonous than WHO standards recommend, and an entire generation of children in Mexico City may be intellectually stunted by lead poisoning (Brown et al., 1991).

Since the Club of Rome's 1972 *Limits to Growth*, the constraints have shifted from source limits to sink limits. Source limits are more open to substitution and are more localized. Since then, the case has substantially strengthened for limits to throughput growth. There is a wide variety of limits. Some are tractable and are being tackled, such as the CFC phase–out under the Montreal Convention. Other limits are less tractable, such as the massive human appropriation of biomass (see below). The key limit is the sink constraint of fossil–energy use. Therefore, the rate of transition to renewables including solar energy, parallels the rate of the transition to sustainability. Here the optimists add the possibility of cheap fusion energy by the year 2050. We are agnostic on technology, and want to encourage it by energy taxes (see Daly, Chapter 2). Hitherto, technology has only started to focus on input reduction and even less on sink management, which suggests there is scope for improvement.

Land–fill sites are becoming harder to find; garbage is shipped thousands of kilometres from industrial to developing countries in search of unfilled sinks. It has so far proved impossible for the United States Nuclear Regulatory Commission to find anywhere to rent a nuclear waste site for $100 million per year. Germany's Kraft–Werk Union signed an agreement with China in July 1987 to bury nuclear waste in Mongolia's Gobi desert. These facts prove that land–fill sites and toxic dumps — aspects of sinks — are increasingly hard to find, that limits are near.

First evidence: human biomass appropriation

The best evidence that there are other imminent limits is the calculation by Vitousek et al. (1986) that the human economy uses — directly or indirectly — about 40 per cent of the net primary product of terrestrial photosynthesis today. (This figure drops to 25 per cent if the oceans and other aquatic ecosystems are included). And desertification, urban encroachment on to agricultural land, blacktopping, soil erosion and pollution are increasing — as is the population's search for food. This means that in only a single doubling of the world's population (say thirty five years) we will use 80 per cent, and 100 per cent shortly thereafter. As Daly (1991*a*, 1991*b*) points out, 100 per cent appropriation is ecologically impossible and socially highly undesirable. The world will go from half empty to full in one doubling period, irrespective of the sink being filled or the source being consumed. Those refusing to recognize overfulness, which has appropriated 40 per cent for humans already, should decide when between now and 100 per cent they would be willing to say 'enough'. They should state in advance what evidence they will require to be convinced. Although this evidence has not been refuted over the last five years, this single study is so stark that we urge prompt corroboration and analysis of the implications.

Second evidence: global warming

The indications of atmospheric carbon dioxide accumulation are pervasive, as geographically extensive as possible, and unimaginably expensive to cure if allowed to worsen. In addition, they are unambiguously negative and strongly so. There may be a few exceptions, such as plants growing faster in CO_2–enriched laboratories where water and nutrients are not limiting. However, in the real world, it seems more likely that crop belts will not shift with changing climate, nor will they grow faster because some other factor (e.g. suitable soils, water) will become limiting. The prodigious North American breadbasket's climate may indeed shift north, but this does not mean the breadbasket will follow because the rich prairie soils will stay put, and Canadian boreal soils and muskeg are very infertile.

The second evidence that limits have been exceeded is global warming. The year 1990 was the warmest in more than a century of record-keeping. Seven of the hottest years on record all occurred in the last eleven years. The 1980s were 0.5°C warmer than the 1880s; while 1990 was 0.7°C warmer. This contrasts alarmingly with the pre-industrial constancy in which the earth's temperature did not vary more than 1–2°C in the last 10,000 years. Humanity's entire social and cultural infrastructure over the last 7,000 years has evolved entirely within a global climate that never deviated as much as 1°C from today's climate (Arrhenius and Waltz, 1990).

It is too soon to be absolutely certain that global 'greenhouse' warming has begun: normal climatic variability is too great for absolute certainty. There is even greater uncertainty about the possible effects. But all the evidence suggests that global warming may well have started, that CO_2 accumulation started years ago, as postulated by Svante Arrhenius in 1896, and that it is rapidly worsening. Scientists now practically universally agree that such warming will occur, though differences remain on the rates. The United States National Academy of Science warned President Bush that global warming may well be the most pressing international issue of the next century. A dwindling minority of scientists remain agnostic. The dispute concerns policy responses much more than the predictions.

The scale of todays fossil–fuel–based human economy seems to be the dominant cause of greenhouse gas accumulation. The biggest contribution to global warming, carbon dioxide released from burning coal, oil and natural gas, is rapidly accumulating in the atmosphere. Today's 5.3 billion people annually burn the equivalent of more than one tonne of coal each.

Next in importance contributing to global warming are all other pollutants released by the economy that exceed the biosphere's absorptive capacity: methane, CFCs and nitrous oxide. Relative to carbon dioxide these three pollutants are orders of magnitude more damaging, though their amount is much less. Today's price to polluters for using atmospheric sink capacity for carbon dioxide disposal is zero, although the real opportunity cost may turn out to be astronomical.

The costs of rejecting the greenhouse hypothesis, if true, are vastly greater than the costs of accepting the hypothesis if it proves to be false. By the time the evidence is irrefutable, it is sure to be too late to avert unacceptable costs, such as the influx of millions of refugees from low–lying coastal areas (55 per cent of the world's population lives on coasts or estuaries), damage to ports and coastal cities, increase in storm intensity, and worst of all, damage to agriculture. And best of all, abating global warming may save money, not cost it, when the benefit from lower fuel bills is factored in (Lovins, 1990). The greenhouse threat is more than sufficient to justify action now, even if only as an insurance.

The relevant component here is the tight relationship between carbon released and the scale of the economy. Global carbon emissions have increased annually since the industrial revolution; now at nearly 4 per cent per annum. To the extent energy use parallels economic activity, carbon emissions are an index of the scale of the economy. Fossil fuels account for 78 per cent of United States energy. Of course there is tremendous scope for reducing the energy intensity of industry and of the economy in general, which is why reductions in carbon emissions are possible without reducing standards of living. A significant degree of decoupling economic growth from energy throughput appears substantially achievable. Witness the 81 per cent increase in Japan's output since 1973 using the same amount of energy. Similarly, the United States' near 39 per cent increase in GNP since 1973, but with only modest increase in energy use. This means energy efficiency increased almost 26 per cent. Sweden — cold, gloomy, industrialized and very energy efficient — is the best example of how profitable it can be to reduce CO_2. The Swedish State Power Board found that doubled electric efficiency, 34 per cent decrease in CO_2, phase out of the nuclear power which supplies 50 per cent of the country's electricity, actually *lowers* consumers' electricity bills by \$1 billion per year (Lovins, 1990). Other, less efficient nations should be able to do even better.

Reducing energy intensity is possible in all industrial economies and in the larger developing economies, such as China, Brazil and India. The scope of increasing energy use without increasing CO_2 means primarily the overdue transition to renewables: biomass, solar, hydro. The other major source of carbon emissions — deforestation — also parallels the scale of the economy. More people needing more land push back frontiers. But there are diminishingly few geopolitical frontiers left today.

Global warming is a compelling argument that limits have been exceeded because it is globally pervasive, rather than disrupting the atmosphere in the region where the CO_2 was produced. In comparison, acid rain, which is damaging parts of the United States and Canada, as well as those parts of Scandinavia downwind from the United Kingdom, and the 'Waldesterben' or 30 billion–dollar loss of much of Europe's forest are more regional evidence for limits.

The nearly 7 billion tonnes of carbon released to the atmosphere each year by human activity (from fossil fuels and deforestation) accumulate in the atmosphere, which suggests that the ecosystem's sinks capable of absorbing carbon have been exceeded, and carbon accumulation appears for all practical purposes irreversible on any relevant time frame, hence it is of major concern for sustainability for future generations. Removal of carbon dioxide by liquefying it or chemically scrubbing it from the stacks might double the cost of electricity. Optimistically, technology may reduce this cost, but still at a major penalty.

Third evidence: ozone shield rupture

The third evidence that global limits have been reached is the rupture of the ozone shield. It is difficult to imagine more compelling evidence that human activity has already damaged our life–support systems than the cosmic holes in the ozone shield. That CFCs would damage the ozone layer was predicted as far back as 1974 by Sherwood Rowland and Mario Molina. But when the damage was first detected — in 1985 in Antarctica — disbelief was so great that the data were rejected as coming from faulty sensors. Retesting and a search of hitherto undigested computer print–outs confirmed that not only did the hole exist in 1985, but that it had appeared each spring since 1979. The world had failed to detect a vast hole that threatened human life and food production and that was more extensive than the United States and taller than Mount

Everest (Shea, 1989). All subsequent tests have proved that the global ozone layer is thinning far faster than models predicted.

The relationship between the increased ultraviolet B radiation let through the impaired ozone shield and skin cancers and cataracts is relatively well known — every 1 per cent decrease in the ozone layer results in 5 per cent more of certain skin cancers — and alarming in neighbouring regions (e.g. Queensland). The world seems set for a billion additional skin cancers, many of them fatal, among people alive today. The possibly more serious human health effect is depression of our immune systems, increasing our vulnerability to an array of tumors, parasites and infectious diseases. In addition, as the shield weakens, crop yields and marine fisheries decline. But the gravest effect may be the uncertainty, such as upsetting normal balances in natural vegetation. Keystone species — those on which many others depend for survival — may decrease leading to widespread disruption in environmental services and accelerating extinctions.

The million or so tonnes of CFCs pumped annually into the biosphere take about ten years to waft up to the ozone layer, where they destroy it with a half–life of 100 to 150 years. The tonnage of CFCs and other ozone–depleting gases released into the atmosphere is increasing damage to the ozone shield. Today's damage, though serious, only reflects the relatively low levels of CFCs released in the early 1980s. If CFC emissions cease today, the world still will be gripped in an unavoidable commitment to ten years of increased damage. This would then gradually return to pre–damage levels over the next 100–150 years.

This seems to be evidence that the global ecosystem's sink capacity to absorb CFC pollution has been vastly exceeded. The limits have been reached and exceeded, humankind is in for damage to environmental services, human health and food production. This is a good example because 85 percent of CFCs are released in the industrial North, but the main hole appeared in the ozone layer 20 kilometres above Antarctica, showing the damage to be widespread and truly global in nature.

Fourth evidence: land degradation

Land degradation, decreased productivity such as caused by accelerated soil erosion, salination and desertification, is only one of the many topics that could be included here. It is not new; land degraded thousands of years ago (e.g. Tigris–Euphrates) remains unproductive today. But the scale has mushroomed and is important because practically 97 per cent of our food comes from land rather than from aquatic or ocean systems. As 35 per cent of the earth's land already is degraded, and as this figure is increasing and largely irreversible in any time–scale of interest to society, such degradation is a sign that we have exceeded the regenerative capacity of the earth's soil source.

Pimentel et al. (1987) found soil erosion to be serious in most of the world's agricultural areas, and that this problem is worsening as more marginal land is brought into production. Soil loss rates, generally ranging from 10 to 100 t/ha/yr, exceed soil formation rates by at least tenfold. Agriculture is leading to erosion, salination or waterlogging of possibly 6 million hectares per year: 'a crisis seriously affecting the world food economy'.

Exceeding the limits of this particular environmental source function raises food prices, and exacerbates income inequality, at a time when 1 billion people are already malnourished. As one third of developing country populations now faces fuel-wood deficits, crop residues and dung are diverted from agriculture to fuel. Fuel-wood overharvesting and this diversion intensify land degradation, hunger and poverty.

Fifth evidence: biodiversity

The scale of the human economy has grown so large that there is no longer room for all species in the Ark. The rates of take-over of wildlife habitat and of species extinctions are the fastest they have ever been in recorded history and are accelerating. The world's richest species habitat, tropical forest, has already been 55 per cent destroyed, the current rate exceeds 168,000 km per year. As the total number of species extant is not yet known to the nearest order of magnitude (5 million or 30 million or more), it is impossible to determine precise extinction rates. However, conservative estimates put the rate at more than 5,000 species of our inherited genetic library irreversibly extinguished each year. This is about 10,000 times as fast as pre–human extinction rates. Less conservative estimates put the rate at 150,000 species per year (Goodland, 1991). Many find such anthropocentrism to be arrogant and immoral. It also increases risks of overshoot. Built-in redundancy is a part of many biological systems, but we do not know how near thresholds are. Most extinctions from tropical deforestation (e.g. colonization) today increase poverty — tropical rain-forest soils are fragile — so we do not even have much of a beneficial trade–off with development here.

Population

Brundtland is sensible on population: getting enough food is too expensive for a quarter of the earth's population today. Birth–weight is declining in places. Poverty stimulates population growth. Direct poverty alleviation is essential; business as usual on poverty alleviation is immoral. MacNeill (1989) states plainly that reducing rates of population growth is an essential condition to achieve sustainability. This is as important, if not more so, in industrial countries as it is in developing countries. Industrial countries have per capita overconsumption, hence overpollution, so are responsible for by far the largest share of limits being reached. The richest 20 per cent of the world consumes over 70 per cent of the world's commercial energy. Thirteen nations already have achieved zero population growth, so it is not utopian to expect others to follow.

Developing countries contribute to exceeding limits because they are so populous today (77 per cent of the world's total), and increasing far faster than their economies can sustain them (90 per cent of world population growth). Real incomes are declining in some areas. If left unchecked, it may be half way through the twenty–first century before the number of births falls back even to today's high levels. Developing countries' population growth alone would account for a 75 per cent increase in their commercial energy consumption by 2025, even if per capita consumption remained at current inadequate levels (OTA, 1991). These countries need so much scale growth that this can only be freed by the transition to sustainability in industrial countries.

The poor must be given the chance, must be assisted, and will justifiably demand to reach at least minimally acceptable li-ving standards by access to the remaining natural resource base. When industrial nations switch from input growth to qualitative development, more resources and environmental functions will be available for the South's needed growth. This is a major role of the World Bank. It is in the interests of developing countries and the world commons not to follow the fossil fuel model. It is in the interest of industrial countries to subsidize alternatives, and this is an increasing role for the World Bank. This view is repeated by Dr Qu Wenhu of the Academica Sinica who says: 'if "needs" includes one automobile for each of a billion Chinese, then sustainable development is impossible'. Developing populations account for only 17 per cent of total commercial energy now, but unchecked this will almost double by 2020 (OTA, 1991).

Merely meeting unmet demand for family planning would help enormously. Educating girls and providing them with credit for productive purposes and employment opportunities are probably the next most effective measures. A full 25 per cent of American births, and a much larger number of births in the developing countries, are to unmarried mothers, hence providing less child care. Most of these births are unwanted, which also tends to result in less care. Certainly, international development agencies should help high–population– growth countries reduce their population growth rates to world averages as an urgent first step, instead of trying only to increase infrastructure without population measures.

Growth versus development

To the extent the economic subsystem has indeed become large relative to the global ecosystem on which it depends, and the regenerative and assimilative capacities of its sources and sinks are being exceeded, then the growth called for by Brundtland will dangerously exacerbate surpassing the limits outlined above. Opinions differ. MacNeill (1989) claims 'a minimum of 3 per cent annual per capita income growth is needed to reach sustainability during the first part of the next century', and this would need higher growth in national income, given population trends. Hueting (1990) disagrees, concluding that for sustainability 'what we need *least* is an increase in national

income'. Sustainability will be achieved only to the extent quantitative throughput growth stabilizes and is replaced by qualitative development, holding inputs constant. Reverting to the scale of the economy — population times per capita resource use — per capita resource use must decline, as well as population.

Brundtland is excellent on three of the four necessary conditions. First, producing more with less (e.g. conservation, efficiency, technological improvements and recycling). Japan excels in this regard, producing 81 per cent more real output than it did in 1973 using the same amount of energy. Second, reducing the population explosion. Third, redistribution from overconsumers to the poor. Brundtland was probably being politically astute in leaving fuzzy the fourth necessary condition to make all four sufficient to reach sustainability. This is the transition from input growth and growth in the scale of the economy to qualitative development, holding the scale of the economy consistent with the regenerative and assimilative capacities of global life–support systems. In several places the Brundtland report hints at this. In qualitative sustainable development, production replaces depreciated assets, and births replace deaths, so that stocks of wealth and people are continually renewed and even improved (Daly, 1990a). A developing economy is getting better: well–being of the (stable) population improves. An economy growing in throughput is getting bigger, exceeding limits, damaging the self–repairing capacity of the planet.

To the extent that our leaders recognize the fact that the globe has reached limits and decide to reduce further expansion in the scale of the economy, we must prevent hardship in this tremendous transition for poor countries. Brundtland commendably advocates growth for poor countries. But only raising the bottom without lowering the top will not permit sustainability (Haavelmo, 1990).

The poor need an irreducible minimum of basics — food, clothing and shelter. These basics require throughput growth for poor countries, with compensating reductions in such growth in rich countries. Apart from colonial–resource draw–downs, industrial–country growth historically has increased markets for developing countries' raw materials, hence presumably benefiting poor countries, but it is industrial–country growth that has to contract to make ecological room for the minimum growth needed in poor country economies. Tinbergen and Hueting (see Chapter 4) put it plainest — 'no further production growth in rich countries'. All approaches to sustainability must internalize this constraint if the crucial goals of poverty alleviation and halting damage to global life support systems are to be approached.

Conclusion

When there is a change from agrarian through industrial to more service–oriented economies, then smoke–stack throughput growth may improve to growth less damaging of sources and sinks: coal and steel to fibre optics and electronics for example. We must speed to production that is less throughput–intensive. We must accelerate technical improvements in resource productivity; Brundtland's 'producing more with less'. Presumably this is what the Brundtland commission and subsequent follow–up authors (e.g. MacNeill, 1989) label growth, but of a different kind. Vigorous promotion of this trend will indeed help the transition to sustainability, and is probably essential. It is also largely true that conservation and efficiency improvements and recycling are profitable, and will become much more so the instant environmental externalities (e.g. carbon

dioxide emissions) are internalized.

But it will be insufficient for four reasons. First, all growth consumes resources and produces wastes, even Brundtland's unspecified new type of growth. To the extent we have reached limits to the ecosystem's regenerative and assimilative capacities, throughput growth exceeding such limits will not herald sustainability. Second, the size of the service sector relative to the production of goods has limits. Third, even many services are fairly throughput–intensive, such as tourism, universities and hospitals. Fourth, and highly significant, is that less throughput–intensive growth is 'high–tech', hence the places where there have to be more growth — tiny, impoverished, developing–country economies — are less likely to be able to afford Brundtland's 'new' growth.

Part of the answer will be massive technology transfer from industrial countries to developing countries to offer them whatever throughput–neutral or throughput–minimal technologies are available. This transfer is presaged by the $1.5 billion Global Environment Facility of UNEP, UNDP and the World Bank, which is starting to finance improvements not yet fully 'economic', but which benefit the global commons.

This chapter is not primarily about how to approach sustainability, which is well documented elsewhere (Adams, 1990; Agarwal and Narain, 1990; Chambers et al., 1990; Conroy and Litvinoff, 1988; Goldsmith et al., 1990). Nor is it about the economic and political difficulties of reaching sustainability, such as the pricing of the infinite (e.g. ozone shield), endlessly debatable (e.g. biodiversity), or pricing for posterity what we cannot price today. That is admirably argued by Daly and Cobb (1989), Daly (1990*a*, 1991*a*, 1991*b*), El Serafy (1991), and Costanza (1991). It is about the need to recognize the imminence of limits to throughput growth, while alleviating poverty in the world. Many local thresholds have been broached because of population pressures and poverty; global thresholds are being broached by industrial countries' overconsumption.

To conclude on an optimistic note: OECD found in 1984 that environmental expenditure is good for theeconomy and good for employment. The 1988 Worldwatch study (Brown, 1988) speculated that most sustainability could be achieved by the year 2000 with additional annual expenditure increasing gradually to $150 billion in 2000. Most measures needed to approach sustainability are beneficial also for other reasons (e.g. fuel efficiency). The world's nations have annually funded UNEP with about $30 million, although they propose now 'to consider' increasing this sum to $100 million.

Money is available; financial capital shortage no longer limits the economy. It is shortages of both natural capital, and political will in the industrialized world. Yet we fail to follow economic logic and invest in the limiting factor.

Many nations spend less on environment, health, education and welfare than they do on arms, which now annually total $1,000 billion. Global security is increasingly prejudiced by source and sink constraints as recent natural resource wars have shown, such as the 1974 'Cod War' between United Kingdom and Iceland, the 1969 Football War between overpopulated El Salvador and under–populated Honduras, and the 1991 Gulf War. As soon as damage to global life–support systems is perceived as far riskier than military threats, more prudent reallocation will promptly follow. ∎

Acknowledgements

The author wishes to acknowledge the useful comments of Paul Ehrlich, Stein Hansen, Roefie Hueting, Frederik van Bolhuis, Sandra Postel, Jane Pratt and Richard Norgaard.

References

ADAMS, W. M. 1990. *Green Development: Environment and Sustainability in the Third World.* London, Routledge. 255 pp.

AGARWAL, A.; NARAIN, S. 1990. *Towards Green Villages.* Delhi, Centre for Science and Environment. 52 pp.

ARRHENIUS, E.; WALTZ, T.W. 1990. *The Greenhouse Effect: Implications for Economic Development.* Washington, D.C., World Bank. 18 pp. (Discussion Paper, 78.)

BROWN, L. R. 1988. *State of the World.* Washington, D.C., Worldwatch Institute. 237 pp. (See also 1989, 1990 and 1991 editions.)

CATTON, W. R. 1982. *Overshoot: The Ecological Basis of Revolutionary Change.* Chicago, University of Illinois Press. 298 pp.

CHAMBERS, R.; SAXENA, N.C.; SHAH, T. 1990. *To the Hands of the Poor.* London, Intermediate Technology. 273 pp.

CONROY, C.; LITVINOFF, M. 1988. *The Greening of Aid: Sustainable Livelihoods in Practice.* London, Earthscan. 302 pp.

COSTANZA, R. (ed.). 1991. *Ecological Economics: The Science and Management of Sustainability.* New York, Columbia Press. 535 pp.

COURT, T. De La. 1990. *Beyond Brundtland: Green Development in the 1990s.* London, Zed Books. 139 pp.

DAILY, G. C.; EHRLICH, P.R. 1990. An Exploratory Model of the Impact of Rapid Climate Change on the World Food Situation. *Proceedings of the Royal Society,* Vol. 241, pp. 232–44.

DALY, H. E. 1990*a.* Toward Some Operational Principles of Sustainable Development. *Ecological Economics,* Vol. 2, pp. 1–6.

—. 1990*b.* Boundless Bull. *Gannett Center Journal,* Vol. 4, No. 3, pp. 113–18.

—. 1991*a.* Ecological Economics and Sustainable Development. In: C. Rossi. and E. Tiezzi (eds.), *Ecological Physical Chemistry.* Amsterdam, Elsevier.

—. 1991*b.* Towards an Environmental Macroeconomics. In: R. Costanza (ed.), *Ecological Economics: The Science and Management of Sustainability.* New York, Columbia Press. 535 pp.

—. 1991*c.* Sustainable Development: From Conceptual Theory Towards Operational Principles. *Population and Development Review.* (Forthcoming.)

DALY, H. E.; COBB, J. 1989. *For the Common Good: Redirecting the Economy Towards Community, the Environment, and a Sustainable Future.* Boston, Beacon Press. 482 pp.

EHRLICH, P. 1989. The Limits to Substitution: Meta–Resource Depletion and a New Economic–Ecologic Paradigm. *Ecological Economics,* Vol. 1, No. 1, pp. 9–16.

EHRLICH, P.; EHRLICH, A. 1990. *The Population Explosion.* New York, Simon & Schuster. 320 pp.

El SERAFY, S. 1991. The Environment as Capital. In: R. Costanza (ed.), *Ecological Economics: The Science and Management of Sustainability.* New York, Columbia Press. 535 pp.

FOY, G. 1990. Economic Sustainability and the Preservation of Environmental Assets. *Environmental Management,* Vol. 14, No. 6, pp. 771–8.

GOLDSMITH, E.; Hildyard, N.; Bunyard, P. 1990. *5000 Days to Save the Planet.* London, Hamlyn. 320 pp.

GOODLAND, R. 1991. Tropical Deforestation: Solutions, Ethics and Religion. Washington, D.C., World Bank. 62 pp. (Environment Department Working Paper, 43.)

GOODLAND, R.; DALY, H. 1990. The Missing Tools (for Sustainability). In: C. Mungall and D.J.McLaren (eds.), *Planet Under Stress: The Challenge of Global Change.* pp. 269–82. Toronto, Oxford University Press. 344 pp.

GOODLAND, R.; LEDEC, G. 1987. Neoclassical Economics and Sustainable Development. *Ecological Modelling,* Vol. 38, pp. 19–46.

GOODLAND, R.; ASIBEY, E.; POST, J.; DYSON, M. 1991. Tropical Moist Forest Management: the Urgency of Transition to Sustainability. *Environmental Conservation,* Spring.

HAAVELMO, T. 1990. The Big Dilemma, International Trade and the North–South Cooperation. *Economic Policies for Sustainable Development,* Box 1–1; p. 7. Manila, Asian Development Bank. 253 pp.

HARDIN, G. 1991. Paramount Positions in Ecological Economics. In: R. Costanza (ed.), *Ecological Economics: The Science and Management of Sustainability*. New York, Columbia Press. 535 pp.

HUETING, R. 1990. The Brundtland Report: A Matter of Conflicting Goals. *Ecological Economics*, Vol. 2, No. 2, pp. 109–18.

LOVINS, A. B. 1990. Does Abating Global Warming Cost or Save Money? *Rocky Mountain Inst.* Vol. 6, No. 3, pp. 1–3. (Old Snowmass, Colo.)

MACNEILL, J. 1989. Strategies for Sustainable Development. *Scientific American.* Vol. 261, No. 3, pp. 154–65.

MEADOWS, D. H. et al. 1974. *The Limits to Growth: A Report for the Club of Rome's Project on the Predicament of Mankind,* 2nd. ed. New York, Universe Books. 205 pp.

OTA. 1991. *Energy in Developing Countries*. Washington, D.C., United States Congress. 137 pp. (Office of Technology Assessment.)

PIMENTEL, D. et al. 1987. World Agriculture and Soil Erosion. *BioScience*, Vol. 37, No. 4, pp. 277–283.

SHEA, C. P. 1988. *Protecting Life on Earth: Steps to Save the Ozone Layer*. Washington, D.C., Worldwatch Institute, (Worldwatch Paper 87). 46 pp.

SPETH, J. G. 1989. A Luddite Recants: Technological Innovation and the Environment. *The Amicus Journal* (Spring), pp. 3–5.

VITOUSEK, P. M.; EHRLICH, P.R.; EHRLICH, A.H.; MATSON, P.A. 1986. Human Appropriation of the Products of Photosynthesis. *BioScience*, Vol. 34, No. 6, pp. 368–373.

WCED. 1987. *Our Common Future.* (The Brundtland Report). Oxford, World Commission on Environment and Development/Oxford University Press. 383 pp.

2

From empty-world economics to full-world economics

Recognizing an historical turning point in economic development

Herman E. Daly

Introduction

The thesis argued here is that the evolution of the human economy has passed from an era in which human–made capital was the limiting factor in economic development to an era in which remaining natural capital has become the limiting factor. Economic logic tells us that we should maximize the productivity of the scarcest (limiting) factor, as well as try to increase its supply. This means that economic policy should be designed to increase the productivity of natural capital and its total amount, rather than to increase the productivity of human–made capital and its accumulation, as was appropriate in the past when it was the limiting factor. This chapter aims to give some reasons for believing this 'new era' thesis, and to consider some of the far–reaching policy changes that it would entail, both for development in general and for the multilateral development banks in particular.

Reasons the turning point has not been noticed

Why has this transformation from a world relatively empty of human beings and human–made capital to a world relatively full of these not been noticed by economists? If such a fundamental change in the pattern of scarcity is real, as I think it is, then how could it be overlooked by economists whose job is to pay attention to the pattern of scarcity? Some economists, for example, Boulding (1964) and Georgescu–Roegen (1971), have indeed signalled the change, but their voices have been largely unheeded.

One reason is the deceptive acceleration of exponential growth. With a constant rate of growth the world will go from half full to totally full in one doubling period — the same amount of time that it took to go from 1 per cent full to 2 per cent full. Of course the doubling time itself has shortened, compounding the deceptive acceleration. If we take the percentage appropriation by human beings of the net product of land–based photosynthesis as an index of how full the world is of humans and their furniture, then we can say that it is 40 per cent full because we use, directly and indirectly, about 40 per cent of the net primary product of land–based photosynthesis (Vitousek et al., 1986).

Taking thirty–five years as the doubling time of the human scale (i.e. population times per capita resource use) and calculating backwards, we go from the present 40 per cent to only 10 per cent full in just two doubling times or 70 years, which is about an average lifetime. Also 'full' here is taken as 100 per cent human appropriation of the net product of photosynthesis, which on the face of it would seem to be ecologically quite unlikely and socially undesirable (only the most recalcitrant species would remain wild — all others would be managed for human benefit). In other words, effective fulness occurs at less than 100 per cent human pre–emption of net photosynthetic product, and there is much evidence that long run human carrying capacity is reached at less than the existing 40 per cent (see Goodland, Chapter 1). The world has rapidly gone from relatively empty (10 per cent full) to relatively full (40 per cent full). Although 40 per cent is less than half it makes sense to think of it as indicating relative fulness because it is only one doubling time away from 80 per cent, a figure that represents excessive fullness.

This change has been faster than the speed with which fundamental economic paradigms shift. According to physicist Max Planck, a new scientific paradigm triumphs not by convincing the majority of its opponents, but because its opponents eventually die. There has not yet been time for the empty–world economists to die, and meanwhile they have been cloning themselves faster than they are dying by maintaining tight control over their guild. The disciplinary structure of knowledge in modern economics is far tighter than that of the turn–of–the–century physics that was Planck's model. Full–world economics is not yet accepted as academically legitimate; indeed it is not even recognized as a challenge.[1]

Another reason for failing to note the watershed change in the pattern of scarcity is that in order to speak of a *limiting* factor, the factors must be thought of as complementary. If factors are good substitutes, then a shortage of one does not significantly limit the productivity of the other. A standard assumption of neoclassical economics has been that factors of production are highly substitutable. Although other models of production have considered factors as not at all substitutable (e.g. the total complementarity of the Leontief model), the substitutability assumption has dominated. Consequently the very idea of a limiting factor was pushed into the background. If factors are substitutes rather than complements then there can be no limiting factor and hence no new era based on a change of the limiting role from one factor to another. It is therefore important to be very clear on the issue of complementarity versus substitutability.[2]

The productivity of human–made capital is more and more limited by the decreasing supply of complementary natural capital. Of course in the past when the scale of the human presence in the biosphere was low, human–made capital played the limiting role. The switch from human–made to natural capital as the limiting factor is thus a function of the increasing scale and impact of the human presence. Natural capital is the stock that yields the flow of natural resources — the forest that yields the flow of cut timber; the petroleum deposits that yield the flow of pumped crude oil, the fish populations in the sea that yield the flow of caught fish. The complementary nature of natural and human–made capital is made obvious by asking what good a saw mill is without a forest; a refinery without petroleum deposits; a fishing boat without populations of fish.

Beyond some point in the accumulation of human–made capital it is clear that the limiting factor on production will be remaining natural capital. For example, the limiting factor determining the fish catch is the reproductive capacity of fish populations, not the number of fishing boats; for gasoline the limiting factor is petroleum deposits, not refinery capacity; and for many types of wood it is remaining forests, not saw–mill capacity. Costa Rica and peninsular Malaysia, for example, now must import timber to keep their saw mills employed. One country can accumulate human–made capital and deplete natural capital to a greater extent only if another country does it to a lesser extent—for example, Costa Rica must import timber from somewhere. The demands of complementarity between human–made and natural capital can be evaded within a nation only if they are respected between nations.

Of course multiplying specific examples of complementarity between natural and human–made capital will never suffice to prove the general case. But the examples given above at least serve to add concreteness to the more general arguments for the complementarity hypothesis given in the next section.

Because of the complementary relation between human–made and natural capital the very accumulation of human–made capital puts pressure on natural capital stocks to supply an increasing flow of natural resources. When that flow reaches a size that can no longer be maintained there is a big temptation to supply the annual flow unsustainably by liquidation of natural capital stocks, thus postponing the collapse in the value of the complementary human–made capital. Indeed in the era of empty–world economics, natural resources and natural capital were considered free goods (except for extraction or harvest costs). Consequently the value of human–made capital was under no threat from scarcity of a complementary factor. In the era of full–world economics this threat is real and is met by liquidating stocks of natural capital to temporarily keep up the flows of natural resources that support the value of human–made capital. Hence the problem of sustainability.

More on complementarity versus substitutability

The main issue is the relation between natural capital that yields a flow of natural resources and services that enter the process of production, and the human–made capital that serves as an agent in the process for transforming the resource inflow into a product outflow. Is the flow of natural resources (and the stock of natural capital that yields that flow) substitutable by human–made capital? Clearly one resource can substitute for another — we can transform aluminium instead of copper into electric wire. We can also substitute labour for capital, or capital for labour, to a significant degree even though the characteristic of complementarity is also important. For example, we can have fewer carpenters and more

Herman E. Daly

power saws, or fewer power saws and more carpenters and still build the same house. But more pilots cannot substitute for fewer aircraft, once the aircraft are fully employed.

In other words, one resource can substitute for another, albeit imperfectly, because both play the same qualitative role in production — both are raw materials undergoing transformation into a product. Likewise capital and labour are substitutable to a significant degree because both play the role of agent of transformation of resource inputs into product outputs. However, when we come to substitution across the roles of transforming agent and material undergoing transformation (efficient cause and material cause), the possibilities of substitution become very limited and the characteristic of complementarity is dominant. For example, we cannot construct the same house with half the lumber no matter how many extra power saws or carpenters we try to substitute. Of course we might substitute brick for lumber, but then we face the analogous limitation — we cannot substitute bricklayers and trowels for bricks.

The complementarity of natural and human–made capital

The upshot of these considerations is that natural capital (natural resources) and human–made capital are complements rather than substitutes. The neo–classical assumption of near perfect substitutability between natural resources and human–made capital is a serious distortion of reality, the excuse of 'analytical convenience' notwithstanding. To see how serious, just imagine that in fact human–made capital was indeed a perfect substitute for natural resources. Then it would also be the case that natural resources would be a perfect substitute for human–made capital. Yet if that were so then we would have had no reason whatsoever to accumulate human–made capital, since we were already endowed by nature with a perfect substitute. Historically, of course, we did accumulate human–made capital long before natural capital was depleted, precisely because we needed human–made capital to make effective use of the natural capital (complementarity!).

It is quite amazing that the substitutability dogma should be held with such tenacity in the face of such an easy *reductio ad absurdum*. Add to that the fact that capital itself requires natural resources for its production — that is, the substitute itself requires the very input being substituted for — and it is quite clear that human–made capital and natural resources are fundamentally complements not substitutes. Substitutability of capital for resources is limited to reducing waste of materials in process, for example, collecting sawdust and using a press (capital) to make chip–board. And no amount of substitution of capital for resources can ever reduce the mass of material resource inputs below the mass of the outputs, given the law of conservation of matter–energy.

Substitutability of capital for resources in aggregate production functions reflects largely a change in the total product mix from resource–intensive to different capital–intensive products. It is an artefact of product aggregation, not factor substitution (i.e. along a given product isoquant). It is important to emphasize that it is this latter meaning of substitution that is under attack here — that is, producing a given physical product with less natural resources and more capital. No one denies that it is possible to produce a different product or a different product mix with less resources. Indeed new products may be designed to provide the same or better service while using fewer resources, and sometimes less labour and less capital as well. This is technical improvement, not substitution of capital for resources. Light bulbs that give more lumens per watt represent technical progress, qualitative improvement in the state of the art, not the substitution of a quantity of capital for a quantity of natural resource in the production of a given quantity of a product.

It may be that economists are speaking loosely and metaphorically when they claim that capital is a near perfect substitute for natural resources. Perhaps they are counting as 'capital' all improvements in knowledge, technology, managerial skills, etc. — in short anything that would increase the efficiency with which resources are used. If this is the usage then 'capital' and resources would by definition be substitutes in the same sense that more efficient use of a resource is a substitute for using more of the resource. But to define capital as efficiency would make a mockery of the neoclassical theory of production, where efficiency is a ratio of output to input, and capital is a quantity of input.

The productivity of human–made capital is more and more limited by the decreasing supply of complementary natural capital. Of course in the past when the scale of the human presence in the biosphere was low, human–made capital played the limiting role. The switch from human–made to natural capital as the limiting factor is thus a function of the increasing scale of the human presence.

More on natural capital

Thinking of the natural environment as 'natural capital' is in some ways unsatisfactory, but useful within limits. We may define capital broadly as a stock of something that yields a flow of useful goods or services. Traditionally capital was defined as produced means of production, which we are here calling human–made capital in distinction to natural capital, which, though not made by people, is nevertheless functionally a stock that yields a flow of useful goods and services. We can distinguish renewable from non–renewable, and marketed from non–marketed natural capital, giving four cross categories. Pricing natural capital, especially non–marketable natural capital, is so far an intractable problem, but one that need not be faced here. All that need be recognized for the present argument is, that natural capital consists of physical stocks that are complementary to human–made capital. We have learned to use a concept of human capital that departs even more fundamentally from the standard definition of capital. Human capital cannot be bought and sold, though it can be rented. Although it can be accumulated it cannot be inherited without effort by bequest as can ordinary human–made capital, but must be learned anew by each generation. Natural capital, however, is more like traditional human–made capital in that it can be bequeathed. Overall the concept of natural capital is less a departure from the traditional definition of capital is the commonly used notion of human capital.

There is a troublesome subcategory of marketed natural capital that is intermediate between natural and human–made, which we might refer to as 'cultivated natural capital', consisting of such things as plantation forests, herds of livestock, agricultural crops, fish bred in ponds, etc. Cultivated natural capital supplies the raw material input complementary to human–made capital, but does not provide the wide range of natural ecological services characteristic of natural capital proper (for example, eucalyptus plantations supply timber to the saw mill and may even reduce erosion, but they do not provide a wildlife habitat nor do they preserve biodiversity). Investment in the cultivated natural capital of a forest plantation, however, is useful not only for the timber, but as a way of easing the pressure of timber interests on the remaining true natural capital of real forests.

Marketed natural capital can, subject to the important social corrections for common property and myopic discounting, be left to the market. Non–marketed natural capital, both renewable and non–renewable, will be the most troublesome category. Remaining natural forests should in many cases be treated as non–marketed natural capital, and only replanted areas treated as marketed natural capital. In neo–classical terms the external benefits of remaining natural forests might be considered 'infinite' thus removing them from market competition with other (inferior) uses. Most neo–classical economists, however, have a strong aversion to any imputation of an 'infinite' or prohibitive price to anything.

Policy implications of the turning point

In this new full–world era, investment must shift from human–made capital accumulation towards natural capital preservation and restoration. Also, technology should be aimed at increasing the productivity of natural capital more than human–made capital. If these two things do not happen then we will be behaving *uneconomically* — in the most orthodox sense of the word. That is to say, the emphasis should shift from technologies that increase the productivity of labour and human–made capital to those that increase the productivity of natural capital. This would occur through market forces if the price of natural capital were to rise as it became more scarce. What keeps the price from rising? In most cases natural capital is

unowned and consequently non–marketed. Therefore it has no explicit price and is exploited as if its price were zero. Even where prices exist on natural capital the market tends to be myopic and excessively discounts the costs of future scarcity, especially when under the influence of economists who teach that accumulating capital is a near perfect substitute for depleting natural resources!

Natural capital productivity is increased by: (a) increasing the flow (net growth) of natural resources per unit of natural stock (limited by biological growth rates); (b) increasing product output per unit of resource input (limited by mass balance); and especially (c) increasing the end–use efficiency with which the resulting product yields services to the final user (limited by technology). We have already argued that complementarity severely limits what we should expect from (b), and complex ecological interrelations and the law of conservation of matter–energy will limit the increase from (a). Therefore the focus should be mainly on (c).

The above factors limit productivity from the supply side. From the demand side tastes may provide a limit to the economic productivity of natural capital that is more stringent than the limit of biological productivity. For example, game ranching and fruit–and–nut gathering in a natural tropical forest may, in terms of biomass be more productive than cattle ranching. But undeveloped tastes for game meat and tropical fruit may make this use less profitable than the biologically more productive use. In this case a change in tastes can increase the biological productivity with which the land is used.

Since human–made capital is owned by the capitalist we can expect that it will be maintained with an interest to increasing its productivity. Labour power, which is a stock that yields the useful services of labour, can be treated in the same way as human–made capital. Labour power is owned by the labourer who has an interest in maintaining it and enhancing its productivity. But non–marketed natural capital (the water cycle, the ozone layer, the atmosphere, etc.) is not subject to ownership, and no self–interested social class can be relied upon to protect it from over-exploitation.

If the thesis argued above were accepted by development economists and the multilateral development banks, what policy implications would follow? The role of the multilateral development banks in the new era would be increasingly to make investments that replenish the stock and that increase the productivity of natural capital. In the past, development investments have largely aimed at increasing the stock and productivity of human–made capital. Instead of investing mainly in saw–mills, fishing–boats and refineries, development banks should now invest more in reforestation, restocking of fish populations and renewable substitutes for dwindling reserves of petroleum. The latter should include investment in energy efficiency, as it is impossible to restock petroleum deposits.

Since natural capacity to absorb wastes is also a vital resource, investments that preserve that capacity (e.g. pollution reduction) also increase in priority. For marketed natural capital this will not represent a revolutionary change. For non–marketed natural capital it will be more difficult, but even here economic development agencies have experience in investing in complementary public goods such as education, legal systems, public infrastructure and population control. Investments in limiting the growth–rate of the human population are of greatest importance in managing a world that has become relatively full. Like human–made capital, labour power is also complementary with natural resources and its growth can

increase demand for natural resources beyond the capacity of natural capital to sustain supply.

Perhaps the clearest policy implication of the full–world thesis is that the level of per capita resource use of the rich countries cannot be generalized to the poor, given the current world population. Present total resource use levels are already unsustainable, and multiplying them by a factor of 5 to 10 as envisaged in the Brundtland Report, albeit with considerable qualification, is ecologically impossible. As a policy of growth becomes less possible, the importance of redistribution and population control as measures to combat poverty increase correspondingly. In a full world both human numbers and per capita resource use must be constrained. Poor countries cannot cut per capita resource use, indeed they must increase it to reach a sufficiency, so their focus must be mainly on population control. Rich countries can cut both, and for those that have already reached demographic equilibrium the focus would be more on limiting per capita consumption to make resources available for transfer to help bring the poor up to sufficiency. Investments in the areas of population control and redistribution therefore increase in priority for development agencies.

Investing in natural capital (non–marketed) is essentially an infrastructure investment on a grand scale and in the most fundamental sense of infrastructure — that is, the biophysical infrastructure of the entire human niche, not just the within-niche public investments that support the productivity of the private investments. Rather we are now talking about investments in biophysical infrastructure ('infra–infrastructure') to maintain the productivity of all previous economic investments in human–made capital, be they public or private, by investing in rebuilding the remaining natural capital stocks that have come to be limitative. Indeed, in the new era the World Bank's official name, The International Bank for Reconstruction and Development, should emphasize the word reconstruction and redefine it to refer to reconstruction of natural capital devastated by rapacious 'development', as opposed to the historical meaning of reconstruction of human–made capital in Europe devastated by the Second World War. Since our ability actually to re–create natural capital is very limited, such investments will have to be indirect — that is, conserve the remaining natural capital and encourage its natural growth by reducing our level of current exploitation. This includes investing in projects that relieve the pressure on these natural capital stocks by expanding cultivated natural capital (plantation forests to relieve pressure on natural forests), and by increasing end–use efficiency of products.

The difficulty with infrastructure investments is that their productivity shows up in the enhanced return to other investments, and is therefore difficult both to calculate and to collect for loan repayment. Also in the present context these ecological infrastructure investments are defensive and restorative in nature — that is, they will protect existing rates of return from falling more rapidly than otherwise, rather than raising their rate of return to a higher level. This circumstance will dampen the political enthusiasm for such investments, but will not alter the economic logic favouring them. Past high rates of return to human–made capital were possible only with unsustainable rates of use of natural resources and consequent (uncounted) liquidation of natural capital. We are now learning to deduct natural capital liquidation from our measure of national income (see Ahmad et al., 1989).

The new era of sustainable development will not permit natural capital liquidation to count as a income, and will consequently require that we become accustomed to lower rates of return on human–made capital — rates on the order of magnitude of the biological growth rates of natural capital, as that will be the limiting factor. Once investments in natural capital have resulted in equilibrium stocks that are maintained but not expanded (yielding a constant total resource flow), then all further increase in economic welfare would have to come from increases in pure efficiency resulting from improvements in technology and clarification of priorities. Certainly investments are being made in increasing biological growth–rates, and the advent of genetic engineering will add greatly to this thrust. However, experience to date (e.g. the green revolution) indicates that higher biological yield rates usually require the sacrifice of some other useful quality (disease resistance, flavour, strength of stalk).

In any case the law of conservation of matter–energy cannot be evaded by genetics: that is, more food from a plant or animal implies either more inputs or less matter–energy going to the non–food structures and functions of the organism. To avoid ecological backlashes will require leadership and clarity of purpose on the part of the development agencies. To carry the arguments for infrastructure investments into the area of biophysical/environmental infrastructure or natural capital replenishment will require new thinking by development economists. Since much natural capital is not only public but globally public in nature, the United Nations seems indicated to take a leadership role.

Consider some specific cases of biospheric infrastructure investments and the difficulties they present. First, a largely deforested country will need reforestation to keep the complementary human–made capital of saw mills (carpentry, cabinet–making skills, etc.) from losing their value. Of course the deforested country could for a time resort to importing timber. To protect the human–made capital of dams from silting up the lakes behind them, the water–catchment areas feeding the lakes must be reforested or original forests protected to prevent erosion and siltation. Agricultural investments depending on irrigation can become worthless without forested water catchment areas that recharge aquifers.

Second, at a global level enormous stocks of human–made capital and natural capital are threatened by depletion of the ozone layer, although the exact consequences are too uncertain to be predicted. The greenhouse effect is a threat to the value of all coastal and climatically dependant capital, be it human–made (port cities, wharves, beach resorts) or natural (estuarine breeding grounds for fish and shrimp). And if the natural capital of fish populations diminishes due to loss of breeding grounds, then the value of the human–made capital of fishing boats and canneries will also be diminished in value, as will the labour power (specialized human capital) devoted to fishing, canning, etc. We have begun to adjust national accounts for the liquidation of natural capital, but have not yet recognized that the value of complementary human–made capital must also be written down as the natural capital that it was designed to exploit disappears. Eventually the market will automatically lower the valuation of fishing boats as fish disappear, so perhaps no accounting adjustments are called for. But *ex ante* policy adjustments aimed at avoiding the *ex post* writing down of complementary

human–made capital, whether by market or accountant mechanisms, is certainly called for.

Initial policy response to the historical turning point

Although there is as yet no indication of the degree to which development economists would agree with the thesis argued here, three United Nations agencies (World Bank, UNEP and UNDP) have nevertheless embarked on a project, however exploratory and modest, of biospheric infrastructure investment known as the Global Environment Facility, which would provide concessional funding for programmes investing in the preservation or enhancement of four classes of biospheric infrastructure or non–marketed natural capital. These are: (a) protection of the ozone layer; (b) reduction of greenhouse gas emissions; (c) protection of international water resources; (d) and protection of biodiversity.

If the thesis argued here is correct, then investments of this type should eventually become very important in the lending portfolios of development banks. Likewise, the thesis would provide theoretical justification and guidance for present efforts to fund the Global Environmental Facility and its likely extensions. It would seem that the 'new era' thesis merits serious discussion, both inside and outside the multilateral development banks, especially since it appears that our practical policy response to the reality of the new era has already outrun our theoretical understanding of it. ∎

Acknowledgements

The author is grateful to P. Ehrlich, B. Hannon, G. Lozada, R. Overby, S. Postel, B. von Droste and P. Dogsé for helpful comments.

Notes

1. For an analysis of economics as an academic discipline see Part I of Daly and Cobb (1989).

2. The usual Hicks–Allen definition of complementarity and substitutibility is: 'if a rise in the j th factor price, which reduces the use of the j th factor, increases (resp. reduces) the use of the i th factor for each fixed [level of output], i is a substitute (resp. complement) for j' (Takayama, 1985). In a model with only two factors it follows from this definition that the factors must be substitutes. If they were complements then a rise in the price of one of them would reduce the use of both factors while output remained constant, which is impossible. The customary diagrammatic use of two–factor models thus reinforces the focus on substitutibility by effectively defining complementarity out of existence in the two–factor case. In the Leontief model of L–shaped isoquants (fixed co–efficients) the above definition simply breaks down because the reduction in use of one factor inevitably causes a reduction in output, which the definition requires must remain constant. For the argument of this chapter we need appeal only to 'complementarity' in the sense of a limiting factor. A factor becomes limiting when an increase in the other factor(s) will not increase output, but an increase in the factor in question (the limiting factor) will increase output. For a limiting factor all that is needed is that the isoquant become parallel to one of the axes. And for the practical argument of this chapter 'nearly parallel' would also be quite sufficient.

References

AHMAD, Y. J.; SERAFY, S. El.; LUTZ, E. (eds.) 1989. *Environmental Accounting for Sustainable Development.* Washington, D.C., World Bank.

BOULDING, K. 1964. *The Meaning of the Twentieth Century.* New York, Harper & Row.

DALY, H. E.; COBB, J.B. 1989. *For the Common Good.* Boston, Beacon Press.

GEORGESCU–ROEGEN, N. 1971. *The Entropy Law and the Economic Process.* Cambridge, Harvard University Press.

TAKAYAMA, A. 1985. *Mathematical Economics,* 2nd ed., p. 144, New York, Cambridge University Press.

VITOUSEK, P. M.; EHRLICH, P.R.; EHRLICH, A.H.; MATSON, P.A. 1986. Human Appropriation of the Products of Photosynthesis. *BioScience,* Vol. 34, No. 6, pp. 368–73.

3

On the strategy of trying to reduce economic inequality by expanding the scale of human activity

Trygve Haavelmo and Stein Hansen

The great dilemma

Sustainable development as advocated in the Brundtland Commission Report (WCED, 1987) requires a rate of global economic growth and a distribution of assets and income that would allow developing countries to achieve a significant per capita increase in disposable income as a basis for achieving alleviation of poverty. Invariably, policy statements to this effect mean a strategy whereby the standards of the poor are lifted towards the level of the well-to-do and to the forms of consumption and investments seen in the industrialized countries today.

Such policy statements appear to be founded on a belief that there are, and will be in the future concerns of society, no serious limits to material growth. The various factors of production, such as natural resources, human–made capital, and labour, are assumed to be substitutable so that a shortage of one does not significantly limit the productivity of another.

At the same time the WCED expresses serious concern about the global consequences of human activity in the way of pollution, exhaustion of resources, and generally the danger of a deteriorating environment that future generations must live in. Such concerns appear to reflect the belief that there are — and will increasingly be — serious limits to growth, that is, some of the key factors of production are complementary rather than substitutable.

More specifically, as Herman Daly (see Chapter 2) has put it, the concern expresses a suspicion that an ever–increasing flow of natural resources input in production processes to sustain the required growth inevitably results in liquidating the natural capital stock that supplies this flow. Human–made capital is made from inputs of labour and natural capital, and serves as an agent along with labour in the process of transforming the resource flow into an utility-yielding output flow. If this very resource flow is reduced or disappears, the productivity of the transformation agents (i.e. human–made capital and labour) is reduced. For example, what is the value of a sawmill without a forest to supply logs, or fishing boats without a fish population to catch? Thus complementarity rather than substitutability between the flow of natural resources on the one hand, and human–made capital on the other, must be recognized as a clear possibility, and considered for inclusion as a fundamental assumption for economic planning. This implies that the very accumulation of human–made capital puts increasing pressure on natural capital stocks to supply an increasing flow of natural resources to sustain the productivity of human–made capital.

The case of natural resource cultivation such as farming illustrates this. Agriculturalists established long ago that the basic principle of farming is to change the local natural system into one which produces more of the goods desired by people. This human–made system is an artificial construction that requires continuous economic inputs obtained from the natural environment to maintain its output level. Much of the farming input is thus nothing but an effort to prevent the established artificial state of the land from declining towards an unproductive (from a human perspective) low-level state; most likely lower than the natural state prior to farming of the land (Ruthenberg, 1980).

Fundamentally, rearrangement of matter is the central physical fact about the economic process. Matter cannot be destroyed in the economic system, it can merely be converted or dissipated. These transformation processes generate wastes some of which can be economically recycled, whereas others cannot. To the extent that nature's capacity to assimilate such wastes is or becomes inadequate, wastes will accumulate. Energy is degraded in these transformations. This means that little by little the capacity to rearrange matter is irrevocably used up. Energy flows also drive the basic physical, chemical and biological life-support systems, such as air, water and soils. It is eventually the capacity of these systems that will limit the scale of human activity, that is, long–term

global economic growth (Haavelmo, 1971).

Sustainable development implies a perspective of several generations or centuries. Clearly, a development where population and per capita use of the planet's finite resources both grow significantly, cannot go on indefinitely. Even if population and the level of economic activity were kept stationary, accumulation of pollutants would grow very rapidly because of the growth of entropy beyond nature's capacity of self repair. Entropy is a concept borrowed, somewhat freely, from physics. The concept as used here can be defined as an index measuring the total accumulated pile of useless or harmful wastes produced by human activities over a relevant span of recent economic history (Haavelmo, 1971).

The politically widely acclaimed WCED-definition of sustainable development invariably implies lifting the bottom rather than lowering the top. Successful achievement of global equity goals, via growth and economic efficiency as conventionally measured in the national income accounts, will contradict the environmental dimensions of sustainable development (Asian Development Bank, 1990). Even the most sturdy ship will eventually sink if the cargo is too big. There is little comfort in the fact that the cargo was optimally allocated and fairly distributed at the time of sinking! (Daly and Cobb, 1989).

To make political difficulties worse, even with wide acceptance that lowering the top is required, continued accumulative strain on the natural resource base would be the likely outcome, albeit at a reduced rate. The development process has a tremendous momentum. It can be likened to a journey. You start out from Manila and your destination is Bali. Instead you head north towards Tokyo. You realize that the direction of travel will not bring you to Bali. Therefore, you reduce your travelling speed, that is, you slow down but you do not change your direction. Although this will postpone your time of arrival in Tokyo, it will not bring you any closer to Bali! (Haavelmo, 1980; Asian Development Bank, 1990).

The technological optimistic view

History is full of technological pessimists. The economists of the nineteenth century saw the natural resource base as a limiting factor that would eventually drive the productivity of the transformative agents — labour and capital — down to a level corresponding to a subsistence standard of living (Blaug, 1962). Some of them predicted the industrial revolution would end as coal mines were exhausted. Most doomsday forecasters did not foresee the ability of society, through human capital formation and organization of societies, to improve human–made capital so as to facilitate an unprecedented rate of natural resource extraction to meet rapidly increasing and diversifying consumer demands, thus yielding very attractive returns on human–made capital and labour in many societies.

Many people today look upon those who warn against pollution and exhaustion of resources as technological pessimists. On the other hand, technological optimism is based on a faith in scientific development and technological progress.

Thoughts from the field of decisions under uncertainty also enter the picture. There is the question of who has the burden of proof; the optimist or the pessimist? Here we find two extreme views. One is that because we do not know for certain that the future will be difficult, why worry? The other view is that we should be concerned about the future because we cannot be sure that it will not be difficult. Both views risk making mistaken predictions. Even if we could estimate the chances of

correct or mistaken predictions, there is the question of which mistake is the more serious? Here there is a strong degree of asymmetry. The irreversible effects of an optimistic reckless policy is likely to be vastly more difficult to cope with than that of a more cautious pessimistic policy (Haavelmo, 1954, 1970; Hansen, 1969).

Technological development — which is qualitative progress and thus fundamentally different from quantitative substitution of human–made capital for natural resources (see Daly, Chapter 2) — could take place along two lines relevant to the issues at stake here. The one line is improvement in the ability to use available resources at any time to produce more and more goods. The other line reduces the negative effects of growing entropy. Possibly technological ability in the methods of producing wanted goods and services could develop faster than the negative effects of growing entropy. Even if the negative effects of entropy kept increasing, conceivably people in the future would prefer twice as many goods as we have today, even if they had to wear gas masks. It is even possible that human tastes and preferences would gradually develop in this direction. But there is a fundamental flaw in this optimistic line of reasoning.

If the development of the production of goods and services has reached a certain level at which entropy grows in spite of cleaning efforts, the further development of the ability to produce goods and services has to go on increasing. If the ability to produce goods and services should level off at a higher level, it is just a question of time for the negative effects of entropy to catch up with development. In other words, one would have to produce goods and services at a steadily increasing rate in order to stave off the growing effects of entropy that would creep up as time goes on (Haavelmo, 1971). Even worse, lowering entropy of the economic subsystem requires increasing the entropy of the rest of the system (environment). Since 'the rest of the system' includes the sun, the inevitable entropy increase can be charged to the solar account, but only for a solar–based economy, not a fossil–fuel–based economy (Daly, 1991).

If we could be sure that this eternal chase is according to the informed preferences of society, there is of course not much to be added. The sacred status of consumer sovereignty is the key in this connection. But to what extent do people know what they are doing in the long run? Or, more profoundly, to what extent is it possible at all for people as individuals to make the choice of their future path of development? (Haavelmo, 1954, 1970, 1971).

The principle of the free market will not provide the answer

As is well known, the free–market mechanism with equilibrium prices has certain optimal properties. But there are many assumptions that have to be fulfilled in order to ensure these properties. A fundamental assumption is that there are no collective (or external) side-effects of production or consumption, in addition to what individuals consider as the immediate product of interest to them. If collective side–effects (externalities) are substantial and important, the classical doctrine of the blessings of free trade simply becomes irrelevant as a guideline for economic policy. This is a conclusion that any serious student of economics can verify by means of standard economic textbook theory.

There are three kinds of side-effects of a collective nature that are important in the present context: (a) the production of immediate pollution in the process of production, or production pollution; (b) the indirect effects of the pollution produced, by consumers as a by-product of their enjoying the goods and services they buy, or consumption pollution; and (c) the negative effects of entropy and its impact on environmental deterioration, or environmental pollution.

Every day we hear complaints from producers that their business would not be profitable if they had to pay for the pollution and environmental deterioration that they cause. We can observe a rapidly growing market for shipping toxic, carcinogenic and other waste materials from production and consumption in industrialized countries to developing countries for dumping or recycling. There the laws and regulations on handling, recycling, dumping and storage are often more lenient than those in industrialized economies, where the negative hazards and crowding effects of the accumulating undesirable waste are becoming too costly for comfort.

Consumers are led to overestimate the value of the goods and services they buy because they take the 'surroundings' or natural environment as something given free in any case. This was already well known from the writings of Pigou (1920). In addition to all this comes the human weakness of preferring present goods to future goods, as was pointed out 100 years ago by von Boehm-Bawerk (1891).

This illustrates the difficulty of relying on individual action to make a wise choice from the point of view of the distant future. It is extremely difficult to modify a free–market system by means of taxes and subsidies in order to take care of all the side-effects not included in the simple free–market framework. Recent economic history is full of illustrations of how it has been found necessary to restrict private market forces by publicly invoked constraints.

The core message from these considerations can be further strengthened by addressing the very important current problem in many countries of providing employment for their labour force. Here the real economic problem has been turned almost on its head. The idea of regular and 'respectable' employment among employees is one of working and receiving income from an employer who can pay the wages because what is produced can be sold profitably in the market place. Individual employees cannot make it their business to decide whether or not what they produce is desirable from a general point of view. According to the principle of consumer sovereignty, if there is a market for what the employee helps to produce, then somebody must prefer the product. Hence it is a good thing. Whatever side-effects employees simultaneously help to produce (e.g. environmental damage) they cannot be blamed for, because their partial influence on such side-effects is infinitesimal when compared with their immediate gain from their work and income.

Will technological advances benefit the strong or the weak?

Two conflicting responses are, first, that advances in technological skill and know-how will benefit the strong more than the weak. If, however, the strong (like other people) are primarily selfish, the outcome widens inequality in the world. This tendency is further exacerbated if those who develop technical advances focus on consumer goods and services for a high standard of living, rather than focusing on more elementary improvements of using the world's resources to benefit the poor.

Second, however, is the possibility that increasing ability to use resources more effectively and reduce pollution could be used to help those who are less fortunate and less able to take care of themselves. The disputed 'trickle down' theory could perhaps lead to such an outcome even with the strong being primarily selfish. It is beyond economic theory to speculate on the final conclusion as to what might be the outcome of such conflicting tendencies.

What kind of North–South trade and aid co-operation?

Governments and individuals have for decades assumed natural resource inputs to be abundant, whereas human–made capital and skilled labour needed to transform the natural resources into useful consumption and investment goods have been considered the scarce factors. A consequence of such perceptions and their penetration into commodity market formation has been the fall in relative raw–material prices in world markets. This has contributed to a widening of the gap between industrialized and many natural resource–dependent developing countries.

Such deterioration has been further intensified as a consequence of the global trend-setting production and consumption patterns of rich countries. Poor countries are then tempted to exhaust their own valuable natural resource stocks at low prices in return for imported machinery and consumer goods. Export is not an end in itself. Export only serves a purpose if it can finance useful imports. Developing countries should realize they must stringently avoid exports they cannot afford. Strategies to enhance exports of many staple agricultural products should be critically revisited. Such goods face low demand elasticities in world markets. Individually, each exporter takes the world market price as given. In the aggregate, however, the simultaneous implementation of such strategies by many drives the price down dramatically as they all reach their production targets. In the end, the export revenue might fall short of paying for the imported machinery, implements, pesticides, etc., required to produce for export. The outcome is financial crisis and reduced capability to service increased debt burdens. Such trade includes not only the sale of non–renewable minerals and harvests from soils, forests and oceans, but an increasing use of poor countries' soils as dumps and recycling sites for undesirable waste from industrial production and consumption.

Although many positive things can be said about liberalizing and thus increasing trade, the structure of trade, as we know it at present, is a curse from the perspective of sustainable development (Asian Development Bank, 1990). A drive for efficient resource use in the presence of significant environmental externalities and other market imperfections, requires full-cost pricing of resources in all applications. This in turn implies a need for substantial intervention at national and supra–national levels into otherwise free–market forces of domestic and international trade. Otherwise countries that practice full-cost internalization would, in the short–run, lose out to countries that did not, in a regime of free trade.

Poor countries should begin to recognize the approaching scarcity of some of their natural resources, and plan their exploitation accordingly. International and national policies pursued in a complex world of conflicting individual and group demands must come to grips with approaching natural resource constraints. The global production structure is rapidly approaching a situation where the relative scarcity of input factors is about to be reversed. Increasingly, it is the sustainable flows from natural resource stock that are becoming the limiting production factors, not human–made capital and skilled labour (see Daly, Chapter 2).

This is clearly indicated by the rapid emergence of the technologically advanced 'intermediate' input category that could be labelled cultivated natural capital,

that is 'green revolution' agriculture, hybrid plantation forests, fish farming, etc. However, such highly efficient artificial natural resources may lack the robust biodiversity dimensions of indigenous natural resources. Although being intermediate between natural and human–made inputs, they are far from perfect long-term substitutes for indigenous natural resources; they are in fact subject to the growth of entropy constraints on economic development identified above as a key growth dilemma.

This emerging new bargaining position is what the poor countries need to prepare for while they still have something to bargain with. This requires preparation of development plans and programmes for what the countries' economic activities should look like in the long run. Structural and sectoral adjustments, including changes in domestic price policies, and international debt management will be important components of plans for sustainable development (Hansen, 1989, 1990).

Aid co–operation with the purpose of assisting poor countries to develop towards the same pattern of polluting consumerism as the West is no contribution to sustainable development. It will result in continued rent transfer from natural resource-endowed developing countries to rich countries supplying the South with machinery for speedier resource extraction, which will result in keeping down their prices of natural resources.

On the other hand, aid co–operation with the purpose of assisting in the development of location specific technologies and patterns of consumption adapted to local, cultural and habitual patterns in order to enhance human development and quality of life in a sustainable way should be strongly endorsed.

Such assistance could serve as an eye-opener to the rich donors, and thus help them in the process towards a sustainable world. One possible way to operationalize the concept of sustainable development in economic planning and aid co–operation is by means of so-called compensatory investments (Pearce et al., 1989).

Already, some power–generating companies in industrialized countries have decided that their long–term prospects will benefit from undertaking measures to counter the environmental impact from increased carbon–dioxide emission. Tree planting at home or in another country, or installation of more energy-efficient devices in poor countries where the costs of reducing emissions are well below those at home, are real world examples. One could foresee virgin tropical forests take on increased financial value to the owners if leased out to preserve biodiversity, to provide a natural and sustainable habitat for indigenous people, or to prevent a reduction in the global carbon sink capacity. This maximum sustainable income would be higher than the present combined financial returns to the owners from first cutting and exporting the logs, and then raising cattle for a few years, before the soils become exhausted. With self-imposed national emission barriers in rich countries, such opportunities could soon provide for new financially and economically sound trade and aid flows. The required institutional changes may be moderate (Bohm, 1990).

The outlook: is there a solution?

No matter how people go about managing this planet and the life on it, there is always a 'solution'. Imagine some extraterrestrial recording entity keeping some sort of record of what humanity does on earth, and the consequences of it, and there will always be something to record. The development might be something like what one would conclude from reading Charles Darwin, that is, development might lead into some ecological balance as far as humankind is concerned, including the catastrophe (from our perspective) that humankind becomes extinct.

What people mean by asking for a solution is presumably something else. This something else is then presumably the following. Certain developments are, from the human perspective, more desirable than others. The human mind being rational is supposed to be able to make a sensible choice between various feasible alternatives when it comes to development. So the question boils down to this: Is there a 'good' solution, or a solution which is acceptable?

At least three formidable assumptions have to be fulfilled in order to get a positive answer to this question. The first is that we have a fairly good knowledge of the consequences of alternative paths of human activities in the future. Knowledge in this respect has probably made quite a bit of progress in recent years. The second condition is that there be an addressee to receive this knowledge and use it. The third condition is that this body or some other internationally accepted body be given the authority and power to choose the future path of development and enforce it.

About the last two conditions to be fulfilled one should have no illusion. Perhaps one should settle for the somewhat cynical answer suggested by some people, namely that the situation on earth as far as crowding, pollution and deteriorated environments are concerned will not be recognized until the actual situation becomes much more precarious than it is today.

This leads to what many might find paradoxical. Rapid growth and successful development as conventionally measured, combined with crowding and high population densities, could result in a menu of very few and very costly options for future development. In contrast, hitherto poor growth performance, low levels of infra-structure investments, slow use of the natural resource base, and a relatively sparse population (even if it is growing rapidly at present) could leave relatively more doors open for the choice between future developments (Haavelmo, 1954). Perhaps this is the flavour of optimism we could present for the peoples of Africa at this time of hardship.

The opportunities regarding possible actions for future sustainable develop-ment are limited and diminishing. It would not at all contribute towards sustainable development if nations continue to do as the bewildered tourist who in the treeless sandy desert encountered a hungry lion: 'But what did you do?' asked his friend afterwards. 'I climbed a tree,' said the tourist. 'But there were no trees around,' said his friend. 'Well, what else should I have done?' said the tourist. (Asian Devel-opment Bank, 1990).

Conclusion

Policies for more equality invariably start off that the standard of the poor be lifted towards the level of the rich. In other words, lifting the bottom rather than low-ering the top. However, rapid growth and successful development as conventionally measured, combined with crowding and high population densities, could result in a menu of very few and costly options for future development. The opportunities regarding possible actions for future sustainable development are limited and diminishing. A 'good' or acceptable devel-opment solution requires the fulfilment of at least three formidable assumptions. The first is that we have a fairly good knowledge of the consequences of alter-native paths of human activities in the future. The second is that there be an addressee to receive this knowledge and use it. The third is that this body or some other internationally accepted body be given the authority and power to choose the future path of development and en-force it. If these simple facts are not recognized there is no more to be said about the sustainability issue, or any other development policy.

■

References

ASIAN DEVELOPMENT BANK. 1990. *Economic Policies for Sustainable Development.* Manila, Asian Development Bank. 253 pp.

BLAUG, M. 1962. *Economic Theory in Retrospect.* London, Heineman. 756 pp.

BOHM, P. 1990. Efficiency Issues and the Montreal Protocol on CFCs. Washington, D.C., WorldBank. 31 pp. (Environment Working Paper, 40.)

DALY, H. E.; COBB, J. 1989. *For the Common Good: Redirecting the Economy Toward Commu-nity, Environment, and a Sustainable Future.* Boston, Beacon Press. 482 pp.

DALY, H. 1991. Personal communication.

GEORGESCU–ROEGEN, N. 1971. *The Entropy Law and the Economic Process.* Cambridge, Harvard University Press. 457 pp.

HAAVELMO, T. 1954. *A Study in the Theory of Economic Evolution.* Amsterdam, North Holland Publishing Co. 114 pp.

HAAVELMO, T. 1970. Some Observations on Welfare and Economic Growth. In: W.A.M. Eltis, F. G. Scott and J. N. Wolfe (eds.), *Induction, Growth and Trade: Essays in Honour of Sir Roy Harrod.* Oxford, Clarendon Press. 376 pp.

HAAVELMO, T. 1971. Forurensningrsproblemet fra et Samfunnsokonomisk Synspunkt [The Pollution Problem from a Global Perspective] *Sosialokonomen* (Norwegian Journal of Economics), Vol. 11, No. 4. (In Norwegian.)

—. 1980. On the Dynamics of Global Economic Inequality. Oslo Institute of Economics, University of Oslo, 7 May (Memorandum.)

HANSEN, S. 1969. Naturvern eller Naturressurser [Natural Resources for Conservation or Economic Growth]. *Sosialokonomen* (Norwegian Journal of Economics) Vol. 23, No. 2. (In Norwegian.)

—. 1989. Debt for Nature Swaps: Overview and Discussion of Key Issues. *Ecological Economics*, Vol. 1, No. 1. pp. 77-93.

—. 1990. Macroeconomic Policies and Sustainable Development in the Third World. *Journal of International Development*, Vol. 2, No. 4, pp. 533-557.

PEARCE, D.; MARKANDYA, A.; BARBIER, E. 1989. *Blueprint for a Green Economy.* London, Earthscan Publications. 192 pp.

PIGOU, A. 1920. *The Economics of Welfare.* London, Macmillan. 830 pp.

VON BOEHM–BAWERK, E. 1891. *The Positive Theory of Capital.* 428 pp.

RUTHENBERG, H. 1980. *Farming Systems in the Tropics,* 3rd ed. Oxford, Clarendon Press. 424 pp.

WCED. 1987. *Our Common Future* (The Brundtland Report). Oxford, World Commission on Environment and Development/Oxford University Press. 383 pp.

4

NP and market prices

rong signals for sustainable economic success that mask
nvironmental destruction

n Tinbergen and Roefie Hueting

ociety is steering by the wrong ompass

he market is rightly considered a mecha-
ism that generates manufactured goods
nd services according to consumer pref-
rence. This mechanism allows culture
nd technology to put into practice in-
entions enriching human life. It works
fficiently and stimulates productivity in-
rease, which is the motor raising the
uantity, quality and diversity of manu-
actured goods thus becoming available to
onsumers.

An effective measure of the level of
production and its changes from year to
ear—the national income—was devised
n the 1930s (Tinbergen, quoted in
lueting, 1980). People working on this
esearch were well aware that national
ncome would not form a complete indi-
ator of economic success (welfare). But
given a fair distribution of income and
perfect competition it no longer matters
what is produced, only how much of it is
produced. Consequently at that time great
value was attached to the compilation of a
series of figures on the total production of
goods and services. In the 1930s, external
effects, like environmental deterioration,
did not yet play an important role.

This situation has changed drastically.
Over the last forty–five years, the period in
which, based on the above reasoning,
growth of national income has been given
the highest priority in economic policy, the
following picture emerges.

The production of manufactured
goods and services has increased
unprecedentedly, but has been accompa-
nied by an unprecedented destruction of
the most fundamental, scarce and consequently economic good at human disposal, namely the environment. This
process has already caused much human
suffering. Much of what are called natural
disasters, such as erosion, flooding and
desertification, is caused by mismanage-
ment of the environment. This process
threatens the living conditions of generations to come. Furthermore, part of the
growth of national income consists of
production increases in arms, alcohol, to-
bacco and drugs. Few people consider this
progress. Part of GNP growth is double
counting. Thus, in the System of National
Accounts (SNA) environmental losses are
not written off as costs, but expenditure for
their partial recuperation or compensation

is written up as final consumption. The same holds true for expenditure on victims of traffic accidents and diseases caused by consumption, such as smoking.

Increase in production is distributed very unequally. In rich countries, people are led to consume more because of seductive billion–dollar advertising campaigns. But 20 per cent of the population in poor countries are deprived of basic needs, such as adequate food, shelter, potable water, taps and toilets. Economic research has shown that once basic needs have been met, relative income has a greater impact on welfare than absolute income. Finally, production increase has not prevented persistence of high unemployment world–wide and considerable child labour.

The market works well, but not all factors contributing to human welfare are captured by it. Consequently, market prices and economic indicators based on them, such as national income and cost–benefit analyses, send misleading signals to society and therefore must be corrected. The factor for which correction is most urgently needed is the environment.

The relationship between growth and environmental destruction

Environmental degradation is a consequence of production and its growth. The burden on the environment is determined by the number of people, the amount of activity per person and the nature of that activity. These three factors are all reflected in the level of national income. The increase and decrease of the first two burdening factors — population and per capita activity — parallel the increase and decrease of production levels. For the third factor (the nature of our activities) it roughly holds that the more burdensome for the environment our activities are, the higher their contribution is to national income, and vice versa. Thus driving a car contributes more to GNP than riding a bicycle. This emerges from an analysis of the Netherlands national accounts. The sectorial composition of the Netherlands accounts does not differ appreciably from that of the United Kingdom, nor probably from that of most other Northern countries. What follows is therefore by and large valid for industrialized countries.

Production growth results largely from increase in productivity, in which the loss of scarce environmental goods has not been taken into account. Increase in labour volume plays a minor role. A quarter to one third of the activities making up national income (notably state consumption) do not contribute to its growth, because increase in productivity is difficult to measure. Other activities result only in slight improvements in productivity. Average annual growth must therefore be achieved by much higher growth among the remaining activities. Some 30 per cent of activities generate about 70 per cent of growth. Unfortunately, these are precisely the activities which, by their use of space, soil and resources or by their pollution in production or consumption, harm the environment most. These are notably the oil, petrochemical and metal industries, agriculture, public utilities, road building, transport and mining.

Measures to save the environment will have the following effects on growth rates and on production levels. To maintain current life–styles as much as possible, all available technical measures should be applied to the fullest extent affordable. Such measures include end–of–pipe treatment, process–integrated changes, recycling, increasing energy efficiency, terracing agricultural slopes, and sustainably managing forests. Because they require extra input of labour, these measures reduce labour productivity and therefore raise product prices, which in turn checks growth of national income (corrected for double counting). The check of growth can be alleviated by the absorption of unemployed workers, up to the point where full employment has been attained.

Saving the environment without causing a rise in prices and subsequent check of production growth is only possible if a technology is invented that is sufficiently clean, reduces the use of space sufficiently, leaves the soil intact, does not deplete energy and resources (i.e. energy derived from the sun and recycling), and is cheaper (or at least not more expensive) than current technology. This is hardly imaginable for our whole range of current activities. But when such technologies become available, the above mentioned effects will be avoided.

Applying technical measures cannot completely avoid a change in our consumption pattern, because price rises resulting from the measures inevitably cause a shift toward more environmentally benign activities, such as bicycling and using public transport.

Technical measures often do not really solve the problem, either because the growth of the activity overrides the effect of the measure, or because of the persistent and cumulative character of the burden. In this case, the measure only retards the rate of deterioration. Thus, to stop the Netherlands' contribution to acidification of forests and lakes, apart from applying all available technical means, the people in the Netherlands must reduce the number of car–kilometres and farm livestock by about 50 per cent (Fransen, 1987). For some problems no technical measures are available: for instance the loss of habitat of plant and animal species as a result of the use of space, and the formation of cirrus clouds that contribute to the greenhouse effect (CO_2 accumulation may be partly solvable). In these cases, in

addition to the technical measures, a direct shift in behaviour patterns must ensue, forced by do's and don'ts, rules, incentives and taxes.

A direct shift in production and consumption patterns will also check GNP growth as follows from the analysis of national accounts (the environmentally most burdensome activities contribute most to GNP growth). Moreover, in terms of national accounts, environmentally benign activities represent a smaller volume. Thus a bicycle–kilometre represents a smaller volume than a car–kilometre; a sweater a smaller volume than a hot room; an extra blanket a smaller volume than heating the whole house; beans a smaller volume than meat; and a holiday by train, a smaller volume than holiday flights. This is mainly because the exhaustion of environment and resources is not charged to national income as costs. If it were, the differences would become much smaller or nil.

From the above, it follows that saving the environment will certainly check production growth and probably lead to lower levels of national income. This outcome can hardly surprise. Many have known for a long time that population growth and rising production and consumption levels cannot be sustained forever in a finite world. The outcome of the above analysis should arouse optimism rather than pessimism, because environmentally benign activities are remarkably cheap. Thus, a bicycle is much cheaper than a car, a blanket is cheaper than central heating, and rearing two children is cheaper than bringing up ten. This means that saving our planet is indeed possible.

Our fervent goal — to arrive at environmental sustainability, as advocated by the Brundtland Report (WCED, 1987), and by politicians and institutions around the world — can indeed be fulfilled, though only under limiting conditions. In particular, population growth should be avoided as soon as possible. Moreover, activities with little or no material throughput can increase practically forever. As we have seen, this will not result in great increases in national income. Decision–makers should not become upset by this. Changes in national income levels by no means indicate the economic success of their policies because they conceal the destruction of our life support systems, as long as the figures are not corrected for environmental losses.

Correction of national income based on sustainable use of the environment

Attempts to correct national income for environmental losses started in the early 1970s with the following train of thought (Hueting, 1980). The environment is interpreted as the physical surroundings of humanity, on which it is completely dependent (from breathing to producing). Within the environment, a number of possible uses can be distinguished. These are called environmental functions. When the use of a function by an activity is at the expense of the use of another (or the same) function by another activity, or threatens to be so in the future, loss of function occurs. Environmental functions then have become scarce goods, because the use of a function implies, wholly or partly, the sacrifice of another. This fully meets the definition of scarcity that demarcates the economic discipline. This approach links ecology and economics, and places environment centrally in economic theory.

Because national income is recorded in market prices, shadow prices have to be estimated for functions (and their losses) that are directly comparable with prices of manufactured marketed goods. For this purpose, supply and demand curves for functions have to be constructed. It appeared possible to construct supply curves, consisting of the costs of measures eliminating the burden on the environment, arranged by increasing costs per unit burden avoided. But in most cases no complete demand curves can be found. This is because the possibilities for preferences for environmental functions to be manifested via market behaviour are very limited. Other methods, such as willingness to pay or to accept, do not yield complete demand curves, certainly for functions on which current and future life depends. Standard setting was also considered, but the questions of what standards were to be set and by whom could not be answered at that time.

This situation has now changed. Especially after the 1987 Brundtland Report, politicians and organizations worldwide declared themselves in favour of sustainable use of the environment. This preference, voiced by society, opens up the possibility of basing a calculation on standards for the sustainable use of environmental functions instead of (unknown) individual preferences.

Therefore, the following procedure is proposed for correcting GNP for environmental losses (Hueting 1986, 1989). First define physical standards for environmental functions, based on their sustainable use. These standards replace the (unknown) demand curves. Then formulate measures to meet these standards. Finally, estimate the money involved in implementing the measures. The reduction of national income (Y) by the amounts found gives a first approximation of the activity level which, in line with the standards applied, is sustainable. Needless to say a correction for double counting, mentioned above, must also be made. If the sustainable level is Y', the difference between Y and Y' indicates, in money terms, how far society has drifted away from its desired goal of sustainable use of the environment.

The standards can be related to

environmental functions. Thus it is possible to formulate the way in which a forest should be managed in order to attain a sustainable use of its functions. Sustainability then means that all present and future uses remain available. For renewable resources such as forests, water, soil and air, as long as their regenerative capacity remains intact, then the functions remain intact (for example, the function 'supplier of wood' of forests, the function 'drinking water' of water, the function 'soil for raising crops' of soil and the function 'air for physiological functioning' of air). This means that emissions of substances that accumulate in the environment, such as PCBs, heavy metals, nitrates and carbon dioxide, may not exceed the natural assimilative capacity of the environment, and that erosion rates may not exceed natural soil regeneration. As for non–renewable resources, such as oil and copper, 'regeneration' takes the form of research and bringing into practice flow resources such as energy derived from the sun (wind, tidal collectors, photo–voltaic cells), recycling of materials and developing their substitutes.

The measures to meet standards include: reforestation, building terraces, draining roads, maintaining landscape buffers, selective use of pesticides and fertilizers, building treatment plants, material recycling, introducing flow energy, altering industrial processes, using more public transport and bicycles, and use of space that leaves sufficient room for the survival of plant and animal species.

The method is applicable for cost–benefit analyses of projects with long term environmental effects. The method seems to be the only way to confront national income with the losses of environmental functions in monetary terms. The physical data required for comparison with standards come down to basic environmental statistics, which have to be collected in any case if a government is to get a grip on the state of the environment. The formulation of measures to meet standards and estimates of the expenditure involved are indispensable for policy decisions.

In other words, the work for supplementing national income figures might be laborious, but it has to be done in any case if we wish to practise a deliberate policy with respect to the environment. We therefore strongly urge decision–makers to stimulate this kind of research in their countries. The Philippines and Sweden already are interested in following the lead of the Netherlands.

Our debt to future generations

A rough order of magnitude of the debt to future generations the world has been accumulating during the last few decades, and how it is to be paid off, is estimated below. We base this on the use of energy and corresponding CO_2 emissions.

One aspect of sustainability could be that the annual consumption of fuels such as coal, oil and natural gas, expressed as a percentage of known reserves, is equal to the rate of efficiency growth in the use of energy, while keeping the level of production constant (Tinbergen, 1990). Tinbergen found that a figure for this efficiency growth close to reality is 1.67 per cent. By this behaviour, it would be theoretically possible to use a finite stock for an infinite period of time. However, it is not certain whether this will be feasible, because it would mean that the production and consumption of today's package of goods has to be generated with an ever smaller amount of energy. Thus after 315 years, today's package must be generated with 0.5 per cent of today's energy use. 315 years is a short period in relation to the speed of natural processes in question when addressing environmental sustainability.

Therefore, if we also want to avoid the hazards of nuclear energy, development of new technologies such as flow energy (derived from the sun) is less risky.

To avoid greenhouse risks, global CO_2 emissions are estimated to have to be reduced by 75 to 80 per cent. In the period 1950–1988, CO_2 emissions, energy use and GDP ran parallel. Around 1950 both world GDP and energy use amounted to 25 per cent of the 1988 level. This means that, other things being equal, the GDP level must be reduced by 75 per cent. Assuming that a CO_2 reduction of 25 per cent is possible at low cost, and considering that a number of environmental effects are not eliminated by reduced energy use, we conclude that to pay off global environmental debt we would have to halve the level of global activities. This demonstrates the urgency of allocating all available resources, such as know–how and capital, towards the development of new technologies (such as flow energy and recycling), instead of towards increasing production, while halting and then reversing population growth. The last thing the world can afford is to wage war, such as that in the Gulf.

The outlook of such changes in technology seems to be promising. For example, Potma (1990) shows that techniques like splitting water molecules by solar energy in deserts and transporting the resulting hydrogen fuels, can provide the world with sufficient clean energy at twice current energy prices. Desertic developing countries thus have a major export potential. This would allow a sustainable use of the environment while regaining current production levels in 50 to 100 years. This is because sufficient clean energy would become available for both eliminating some environmental effects other than the greenhouse effect and compensating for the necessary decrease in production where no solutions are available with additional production of another kind. Moreover, room would be created for raising per capita production levels in the South by a factor of 2.5. This would reduce the income gap between rich and poor countries from 10:1 to 4:1, with the condition of no further throughput growth in rich countries.

The uncertainties are, of course, far too great to attach great value to the outcome of this scenario. But the above clearly demonstrates that continuing prevailing growth paths is blocking our chances of survival, for which possibilities still remain.

Conclusion

In order to achieve sustainable use of the environment, we conclude that the highest priority should be accorded to devising and implementing economic policies that: (a) accelerate development of new technologies, such as flow energy and recycling; (b) permit no further production growth in rich countries; (c) stabilize the global population as soon as possible; (d) improve international income distribution. ■

References

FRANSEN, J. T. P. 1987. *Zure Regen: Een Nieuw Beleid.* Utrecht, Natuur en Milieu Foundation. 27 pp.

HUETING, R. 1980. *New Scarcity and Economic Growth.* New York, Oxford University Press. 269 pp.

—. 1986. A Note on the Construction of an Environmental Indicator in Monetary Terms as a Supplement to National Income with the Aid of Basic Environmental Statistics. Jakarta, Ministry of Population and Environment. 10 pp. (Mimeo, available from the author.)

—. 1989. Correcting National Income for Environmental Losses: Towards a Practical Solution. In: Y. Ahmad, S. El Serafy and E. Lutz (eds.), *Environmental Accounting for Sustainable Development,* pp. 32–9, Washington, D.C., World Bank. 100 pp.

POTMA, T. G. 1990. Interrelationships Between Environment, Energy and Economy (A paper for the Dutch National Energy Authority). Delft, Center for Energy Conservation and Clean Technology. 17 pp. (Unpublished MS.)

TINBERGEN, J. 1990. Le Incognite del Terzo Millenio. *Dimensione Energia* (Rome), Vol. 38, January/February, pp. 36–41.

—. 1990. How to Leave Enough Natural Resources for Future Generations. *NRC Handelsblad,* p. 8, 22 June. (In Dutch.)

—. 1991. Personal communication, and quoted in Hueting, R. 1980, pp. 153 and 157.

WCED, 1987. *Our Common Future.* (The Brundtland Report). Oxford, World Commission on Environment and Development/Oxford University Press. 383 pp.

5

Sustainability, income measurement and growth

Salah El Serafy

Sustainability

Sustainability is a concept that has figured prominently in the Brundtland Report, though it has proved difficult to define without ambiguity. Within the Brundtland Report itself we find more than one definition, but the one that has since been most quoted is the following: 'Sustainable development is development that meets the needs of the present without compromising the ability of future generations to meet their own needs.' (WCED, 1987). The Report goes on to clarify sustainable development namely: 'It contains within it two key concepts:

- the concept of 'needs', in particular the essential needs of the world's poor, to which overriding priority should be given; and
- the idea of limitations imposed by the state of technology and social organization on the environment's ability to meet present and future needs.'

The reference to limitations of technology and social organization, and to meeting 'essential needs of the world's poor' in the above quotation, and a later statement that 'concern for

social equity between generations . . . must logically be extended to equity within each generation', while appealing to many readers, emphasizes the complexity of Brundtland's sustainability, both as a concept and as a pragmatic guide to policy action. As discussed later in this chapter, the 'vagueness' of definition of Brundtland's sustainability should not detract from its valid concern over addressing distributional issues, which are viewed rightly as an integral part of the environmental problem. This ambiguity is by no means confined to Brundtland. A more recent attempt to clarify what sustainability meant to different authors yielded a bewildering array of definitions (Pezzy, 1989).

The search for a precise meaning of sustainability has remained elusive, and now there is a growing awareness that for practical purposes sustainability should be perceived in approximate terms only. [1] It is certainly evident that the use of the expression 'sustainable growth' has become more frequent in recent development literature, replacing the older unqualified 'growth', in an apparent attempt to impart the notion that growth should be kept within environmental limits. The Brundtland Report represents one of the early attempts at this usage. It is true, however, that such environmental limits remain undefined in a manner conducive to practicable policy guidelines, but I return to this point later.

The impact of Brundtland

In retrospect it seems that although the Brundtland Report made a great impact on world leaders and environmentalists alike, its impact on economists has been rather modest. This is not to deny, however, the influence it has had on economic policy, indirectly through the political forces it has motivated. [2] The attention that has been given to global environmental issues since the publication of *Our Common Future* may be a product of its political impact. [3] There is also the growing coverage of environmental issues in economic work practically everywhere, which may be traced back, at least in part, to Brundtland's publication.

Environmental accounting for sustainable development

While Brundtland was in gestation, an initiative was developing, spurred by the United Nations Environment Programme (UNEP) and the World Bank, to revise national income calculations in order to reflect in them environmental concerns. The coincidence in timing is remarkable between the WCED, which began its work in December 1983 and reached its conclusions in mid–1987, and the UNEP–World Bank workshops that sought improved national income measurements. This parallel effort also began in 1983, reached a crucial stage in 1988, and is still progressing in a number of directions. [4]

Over the past two decades most countries have been calculating their national income according to guidelines, issued in 1968 by the United Nations Statistical Office, generally known as the System of National Accounts (SNA). These guidelines paid practically no attention to the fact that, in order to reckon income properly, the SNA must account for natural resource erosion and environmental degradation. The old system treated much of the anti–pollution expenditures as final expenditures that would raise income, instead of regarding them as necessary intermediate costs that should be charged against the final products. It also failed to take account of environmental disasters when they occurred. It treated natural resources, particularly those emanating from the public sector, as a free gift from nature, reflecting in the accounts mainly their direct extraction costs and any valuation, over and above extraction cost, that the uneven and heterogeneous free market deigned to attach to them.

Worst of all the SNA failed to distinguish between value added by factors of production and sale of natural assets, such as forestry products and petroleum. Through income measurements patterned on the SNA, many natural resource–based developing countries were made out to have a higher income than they actually had, and to be growing at rates that obscured their true economic performance. Furthermore, the accounts failed to reflect the fact that the current levels of prosperity they were enjoying could not last since the basis for such prosperity was progressively being eroded.

False accounting resulted from mixing in the flow accounts elements of natural capital that should have been kept separate from current income. Such income measurements, where they occurred, covered up economic weaknesses that needed urgent attention, thus misdirecting economic policy. Countries where natural resources contributed significantly to fiscal and external balance failed to make essential adjustments and ended up with allocating to consumption too much of the receipts they obtained from selling their natural assets. Many of them took on too much external debt for their own good. Domestically, relative prices moved against tradeable goods, resulting in a lamentable shrinkage of non–natural resource–based activities. It is little wonder that so many resource–rich developing countries that should have benefited from the exceptional improvement of their terms of trade in the 1970s found themselves in the 1980s hardly better off than they had been before (Gelb et al., 1988).

At the UNEP–World Bank workshop held in Paris in November 1988, experts from various national statistical offices met with economists and others who had been investigating the topic of environmental national accounting, and for the first time a consensus was reached that natural resources and the environment were indeed important and likely to become more so in future; that national accounts should reflect the stress on the environment that had become increasingly evident; and that a set of environmental satellite accounts needed to be elaborated and attached to the new SNA core accounts, with the view of reflecting environmental considerations.

That 1988 meeting was a watershed from which significant developments were to flow. Further work since then, conducted in co–operation with the United Nations Statistical Office, has led to the acceptance of the notion that when the revised SNA, expected in 1993, comes out it would recommend compiling a set of satellite environmental accounts showing to the extent possible the changes that occur from year to year in the state of the environment, and attempting a recalculation of national income to reflect such changes. This national accounting adjustment initiative, which still continues, has provided a bridge between some of the objectives of environmentalists and the work of economists.

Sustainability and income

If properly measured, income is sustainable by definition. From an environmental angle errors in measuring income can be viewed as coming largely from wrongly mixing in income certain elements of natural capital, and from confusion of inventory liquidation with depreciation of fixed assets.[5] A person or a nation cannot continue to live at the same material level if present enjoyment is obtained at the cost of liquidating capital. As capital is eroded, the ability to maintain the same level of consumption into the future is undermined. That is why, from its inception, the accounting profession has insisted that for profit and loss calculations, whether for individuals or corporations, capital must be 'kept intact'.

To the accountant, keeping capital intact never meant that capital should be preserved in its original state (the preservationist argument), but only that allowance be made out of current income in order to restore capital to the extent it has eroded. Unless capital is 'maintained', future income would inevitably decline. By extension of the same argument to the area of national accounting, keeping capital, including environmental capital, intact for accounting purposes, requires adjusting income to reflect capital deterioration. Again, this does not mean that the accountant is advocating that capital should be kept undisturbed or, in the language of some environmentalists, that it should be 'preserved' in its existing state, since the very essence of sustaining economic activity relies on using capital to generate future profits or income. There is little disagreement now on extending the same principles that apply to human–made capital to environmental capital, save on the application of those principles to the special case of resources that cannot be renewed or recycled, but whose stock steadily dwindles as it is used up in the productive process.

That the environment can be viewed as natural capital is easy to perceive, both as a sink for wastes and a source of materials and energy (El Serafy, 1991). Wastes have been dumped in rivers and seas, buried on land and dispersed in the atmosphere, in the belief that such natural receptors had an unlimited capacity to receive them. As production has grown, this capacity has clearly been seen to be limited, and has also become limiting. There is thus growing acceptance of the notion that the polluting activities should bear the full costs to society of their pollution. If standards are set for acceptable levels of pollution, the cost of achieving such standards, even if not actually incurred, can be used as a measure of environmental deterioration on account of pollution, and be charged against income as depreciation.

As a source of materials, the environment should also be brought into income calculation. A distinction is clearly needed between resources that can be regenerated and others that cannot. Nature, and society in co–operation with nature, can amend, restore or regenerate fish stocks, forests, soils and the like. Where such regeneration falls short of theoretical or practical rates that would maintain such capital intact (i.e. at its original level at the beginning of each accounting period) shortfalls should be deducted, as depreciation, from gross income calculations. Some problems of valuation would present themselves, but the guiding principle throughout should be pragmatism and approximation since precise measurement is still, and likely to remain,

an unattainable goal. Ecologists, likewise, should attempt measurements of sustainable yield in the same spirit of providing pragmatic and prudential estimates, instead of letting their quest for precision become an obstacle that would render their measurements irrelevant for policy.

In respect of depletable minerals such as fossil fuels, which cannot be meaningfully restored once they are used, applying the same approach of depreciation as in the case of renewable resources would be inappropriate. Such resources represent known wealth that can be liquidated over a variable time span depending on their owners' needs, their expectations of future prices and the state of the market. While productive capacity is depreciated, existing inventories are used up or liquidated, and it would be wrong conceptually to include the proceeds from selling inventories in gross income. And it is equally wrong to believe that, in order to correct for their inclusion in gross income, all that is needed is to deduct the decline of the stock from the wrongly calculated gross income to arrive at a correctly measured net income.

If such an approach is adopted, neither the gross nor the net income will be correctly measured. The gross will be inflated by asset sales that do not represent value added, and the net will be underestimated since the whole contribution of the exploitation activity to income is removed as capital consumption or depreciation. If, on top of such erroneous accounting we add windfalls from upward re–estimation of reserves, and deduct from income downward adjustments of these reserves, we arrive at very dubious and gyrating estimates of income that are as meaningless as they are useless, either for gauging economic performance or for guiding economic policy. A depletable resource's contribution to income requires special handling.

Accounting for depletable resources

In as much as the reserves of depletable resources are ascertained, they should be treated as inventories, not as fixed capital. Inventories can be drawn down to exhaustion if that is perceived by their owners as economically desirable. The proceeds from their exploitation in any one accounting period should, as a first step, be viewed as proceeds from asset sales not as value added. If the owners draw down all their known reserves in one year because they believe this to be best in the light of their assessment of future prices, it would obviously be wrong to include all such proceeds in their gross income for that year, and to deduct the diminution of the asset, equivalent to the same amount that had been included in gross income, so that net income from this activity is shown as zero. Now that the owners have substituted for the subsoil asset, say, a bank account, true income is the interest that can be earned on the new account. Alternatively the owners may sink the proceeds from selling the mineral assets in new material investments whose returns would represent true income. In this way capital liquidation would be kept, as it should, outside the flow accounts.

Following a proposition by the late professor Sir John Hicks, which he put forward half a century ago (Hicks, 1939), it was possible to calculate that part of the proceeds from a wasting asset that must be reinvested in alternative assets so that the yields obtained from such re-investments would compensate for the decline in receipts from the wasting asset. Using a discount rate and the amount extracted from the reserves in any one year relative to total reserves, it was possible to indicate the proportion of the proceeds that can be reckoned as true income, the remainder — a kind of a Keynesian user-cost — having to be set aside and reinvested to produce an aggregate stream of constant future income. The user-cost part is a capital element that should be expunged from gross income (GDP), and therefore would not appear in net income either. If fresh deposits are located, these would affect the flow accounts only indirectly through the change of the reserves–to–extraction ratio, that is, providing a longer lifetime of the asset so that the income part rises and the user cost part falls. [6]

This proposal, which is slowly gaining ground among economists, is still by no means generally accepted, either by them or by the national income statisticians. Many of the latter, even if convinced, would still prefer to preserve old time series of erroneously calculated GDP on the argument that all that is required is to deduct natural resource 'depreciation', equivalent to the entire diminution of stock, from the gross product to show a more sustainable net product which would amount to nil. The conceptual confusion implied by such procedures has already been mentioned. If we must persist with this confusion for the sake of preserving old time series, the user cost, as explained above, would be the appropriate estimate of 'depreciation'.

The limited function of accounting

Accounting by its nature has a limited function. It is essentially a backward-looking activity attempting to sort out from the behaviour of economic units during a past period elements from which an arithmetical history is compiled. This usually takes the form of a snapshot at a point of time (a balance sheet of assets and liabilities), and a flow, during a certain period (most commonly a year), of net results of the economic activity concerned: profits and loss for an individual or corporation, and value added for a nation. Economists have often misunderstood the functions of accountants, and their concern — perhaps obsession — with keeping capital intact, often challenging accountants' meaning of keeping capital intact, and the accuracy of their measurements, since such a concept of capital maintenance inevitably refers to the future.

The Hicksian definition of income itself, whose author insisted that it was merely a rough guide for prudent behaviour, has wrongly been criticized on the economist's usual ground of concern with precision and forward — rather than the accountant's backward — orientation. Hicks's income has been said to be incapable of being 'directly measured' and even that it is 'not suited to an accounting of what happened in the past' either. [8] Whereas Hicks stressed the accountant's quest for approximately defining a level of income that can be devoted to consumption with concern for a sustainability built around the re–use of capital in future, other economists have tended to hanker after a precise level of sustainability, which the Hicksian approach, with its emphasis on *future* income sustainability, obviously cannot meet, partly because the future will always remain unknown.

Economists and accountants have different, but perfectly reconcilable, objectives. In their measurements the accountants seek approximations, assume constant technology, and posit that the future will be a continuation of the past. In practice, technology does change and the future is a little different from the past. But this does not matter much, however, as the accountants' accounting period is seldom more than one year, and every new year brings with it new facts and fresh technology that the accountants have to, and certainly do, take in their stride.

Businesses and governments

The approach I have proposed for estimating income from depletable natural resources, which relies on setting aside part of the proceeds from the sale of natural capital to be sunk in alternative investments so that they may yield a constant stream of future income, begs the question as to what kind of alternative investments are available, and whether for the sake of sustainability such investments will always be available. Here we leave the *ex post* world of the accountant and enter the realm of *ex ante* analysis.

Individual owners of depletable resources usually see to it that part of their receipts, whether in the form of depletable allowances or set–asides, are re–invested so that the owners can continue in business. Whether or not their new investments should be in the same line of business they are already in, or diverted towards other lines, depends on many factors. If the price of the natural resource they own rises to reflect its growing scarcity, thus indicating the opportunity for investment to produce substitutes based on renewable resources, and if such a course is economically feasible, the owners may well continue in the same line of business. But frequently the market would fail to reflect the resource's growing scarcity, and its price would fail to rise. Besides, technologies for producing substitutes may not be available, and if available may not be economic at the prevailing set of prices. Thus we often observe a tendency for diversification away from one–product business on the part of large corporations exploiting natural resources.

Some environmentalists would prefer that the 'user cost' entailed in the exploitation of a depletable natural asset be invested in a 'twin' project that would supply a renewable substitute for the same depletable source. [9] But in the light of the considerations just mentioned, such 'twinning' or 'pairing' may not be attractive to the private owners. On the other hand there is nothing against society as a whole indicating its desire to raise the overall level of savings and investment so that these become consistent with the objective of future income sustainability and also subsidize pioneering and experimental ventures in pursuit of finding renewable sources to replace the diminishing ones. This can be done by insisting, through appropriate monetary and fiscal policies, that the user cost of depletable resource exploitation should be added to current investments. The extra investments would be guided to socially desirable ventures, such as natural resource restoration and maintenance, through a carefully designed system of taxation and subsidies.

User cost and income identities

Consider what happens to the usual identity that income (Y) is the sum total of consumption (C) and investment (I). Denoting user cost by the letter U, we can write:

$$Y = C + I \qquad (1)$$

Adjusting for user cost, equation (1) becomes:

$$Y - U = (C - U) + I \qquad (2)$$

If the user cost is now devoted to fresh investments, income rises and we get:

$$Y = (C - U) + (I + U) \qquad (3)$$

Equation 3 is thus seen to be identical to Equation 1 except that consumption is lower and investment is higher.

Equation 2, however, depicts the correct level of income if the user cost is not reinvested. But if C remains unchanged, then the true level of investment that has been attained is only $I - U$ since U represents a disinvestment. In this latter case we have:

$$Y - U = C + (I - U) \qquad (4)$$

Policy and the problem of scale

Although the approach of sinking part of the proceeds into new investments seems perfectly valid for individuals, businesses and even small countries, which also have the option of acquiring foreign investments if profitable domestic opportunities are not available, can it be workable if it is done on a large scale so that significant portions of global natural capital might be liquidated to be substituted for by human–made capital formation?

Once the problem is posed in this way, the realization of the objective of creating a permanent income stream from wasting assets becomes questionable. Individuals, corporations and even nations can run out of a natural resource — even if their livelihood depended materially on it — in the knowledge that future income may be generated through carefully selected new investments. When considering better accounting for depletable resources my focus was on the income of their owners. It did not matter what form the new investments would take provided they guaranteed for the owners a constant stream of future income. The form of the new investments would be guided by the market, and if the market indicated that the new investments should be in the same line of business, so be it. However, if the problem is considered, not just as one of better accounting for the resource owners, but in a forward context as a guide to economic policy on a global scale, we have to face the issues raised by Brundtland, and the various constraints and propositions we find there for future environmental directions. We also encounter the problems of scale and of ultimate substitutability between natural resources and human–made capital to which Herman Daly has drawn our attention in Chapter 2.

If we perceive the problem globally, then it is clearly necessary to replace say, dwindling natural energy sources, not just by other sources of *income*, but by other sources of *energy* that are renewable, and the issue of 'twinning' becomes relevant. If the market fails to signal rising energy prices to justify investing in renewable energy sources, then society may wish to give the market a helping hand through appropriate policy. Viewed globally, society should have a broad interest in the creation and application of new technologies that would substitute renewable sources for diminishing, non–renewable ones.

But what should be done about the search for an equilibrium between the state of the environment and global economic activity? The world economic organization has been functioning on the basis of economic agents seeking perpetual economic growth, a pursuit that has traditionally been seen not only as desirable for raising material welfare all around, but also as essential for energizing the development of the less developed countries, and thus assisting in the alleviation of poverty. If technology could be organized so that it gave us substitutes for natural resources through the instrument of human–made capital formation, we would be able to continue 'business as usual', hoping that the market would reflect scarcities into higher prices, and thus guide this process of substitution. This certainly appears to be one of Brundtland's fundamental assumptions. However, we have reached a stage where the state of the environment has become so stressed, and

technology and social organization have clearly lagged, at least so far, that some drastic alternative solution deserves to be explored.

Brundtland offered one solution, which leans in favour of maintaining the current emphasis on growth while using the fruits of growth to lessen the material throughput in economic activity, repair the environment, and also for income redistribution, both intra–nationally and from the richer to the poorer nations, with the objective of alleviating poverty. I join with the other contributors in this volume contending that this strategy is questionable, partly because much of the damage to the environment caused by indiscriminate growth is irreversible; partly because the process of substitution of human–made capital for natural resources is slow and erratic; and also in view of the enormous increase projected for global economic activity as compared with the advanced state of environmental stress already reached.

If we are serious about saving our planet, we must seek a steady state for the economies of the rich, while the poor grow and develop so that poverty is eradicated and income disparity, which is the source of so much environmental damage, reduced. Meanwhile technology development and dissemination should be accelerated and population growth urgently halted.

If the Brundtland path is rejected as impractical, can the proposal to arrest growth in much of the world economy be viewed as anything short of utopian? It is difficult specifically to perceive the sociology and political economy of maintaining a steady level of income in the richer countries. Such countries rely primarily on free market forces to guide the allocation of economic resources. In these countries, the essential profit motive is geared unavoidably to business expansion in search of opportunity. The impact of the richer country economic expansion on developing countries has also often been seen as benign in an 'empty world' context of non–binding environmental constraints. In fact every time growth slows down in the richer countries, the poorer ones appear to suffer from depressed incomes and adverse terms of trade. And yet, the richer countries use the bulk of the world resources to support a minority of the world population. If the rich are to grow richer merely to provide markets for the poor, not only are there more economical ways to achieve the same objective, but such a course would accelerate international income inequality.

Clearly something drastic has to take place in social and industrial organization and in the modalities of international relations if a steady state of economic activity, involving a constant level of throughput, is to prevail in the developed countries. Drafting a blueprint for this vision of the future is needed. Its economic content will have to address the problem of obtaining growth and/or development in the poorer countries simultaneously as the economies of the richer countries are kept on an even keel. In addition, the richer countries would be asked to transfer to the less developed countries the resources necessary to redress the negative effect of the richer countries' arrested growth and to alleviate poverty. Furthermore, it is necessary to plan for the kind of economic policy that would have to apply in the richer countries to produce the target of a steady state: as some activities expand, others must contract. What criteria would be used to modulate aggregate activity in a free market economy, which also has to be managed in pursuit of many other policy objectives? The issues this scenario raises will have to be faced by the advocates of such a strategy.[10] The Brundtland Report avoided all these complex issues and opted instead for a non–revolutionary, rather optimistic, but seemingly untenable course.

Conclusion

Finally a word about the importance of proper income accounting since it is income measurements that will indicate what kind of growth or expansion of economic activity is being experienced and projected. Today's income changes, which probably lie behind Brundtland's projections of growth, relate to the GDP as conventionally measured and as valued at factor cost.[11] But if we shift the focus from the gross product to an environmentally more sustainable net product (from which the user–cost of depletable resources has been eliminated), put a value on natural disasters and deduct this from income, and develop the habit of valuing activities at their full environmental cost when prices reflect true scarcities, we are bound to get a very different reading of income and its growth. In which case it might well turn out that the five to ten–times expansion in economic activity, as envisaged by Brundtland and stressed by McNeill (1990), will be less. A hint of this is to be found in the contribution by Tinbergen and Hueting (see Chapter 4), but clearly much work is needed to clarify this issue. ∎

Notes

1. As the reader will note, the search for a precise meaning of sustainability is akin to defining income in exact terms. No unanimity is possible as both concepts rely on our vision of the future. For practical purposes, however, and as a guide for prudent behaviour, we must be content with some useful degree of approximation.

2. Whether it was the Brundtland Report itself, or the political forces that have been gathering momentum independently in various parts of the richer nations, it is remarkable how the impact of the 'Green' movement has been reflected in the declarations of recent economic summits of the Group of Seven industrial nations (G–7) and through the latter's influence has given vent to a number of environmental initiatives. The July 1989 Economic Declaration of the G–7 Economic Summit (Section 37) contained the statements: 'In order to achieve sustainable development, we shall ensure the compatibility of economic growth and development with the protection of the environment. We encourage the World Bank and regional development banks to integrate environmental considerations into their activities'.

3. The July 1990 G–7 Declaration of the Economic Summit referred to global environmental stress (ozone depletion, climate change, marine pollution, and loss of biological diversity) and stated that 'one of our most important responsibilities is to pass on to future generations an environment whose health, beauty and economic potential are not threatened'.

4. It is interesting that in their initial stages the UNEP–World Bank workshops were seeking after setting up national physical indicators of environmental stress, to be combined eventually into one national index, that would reflect the state of the environment, but participants very quickly realized that a system of 'weighting' (or valuation) was necessary to produce such a single index. This moved the concern of the workshops quite early into the direction of reforming national income measurement. See El Serafy (1986).

5. I am abstracting here from a number of activities that have traditionally been excluded from national income reckoning such as household services by family members. That the environment can be viewed as capital, contributing to the productive process, is a notion entirely in harmony with neo–classical economic thinking. See El Serafy (1991).

6. Hicks's all too brief coverage of this topic in *Value and Capital* (Hicks, 1939) shows that he regarded such a user–cost as an allowance for depreciation. In a personal communication in 1987, however, he indicated approval of my line of thinking, and that I had 'made good use of the income chapter in *Value and Capital*'.

7. A qualified acceptance of this approach is to be found in Adelman et al. (1990). This work uses El Serafy's calculations to adjust national income for a number of countries in support of arguments made in the text, but states that 'El Serafy . . . err[s] in supposing that production can proceed at a constant rate then abruptly cease. The decline rate stands at the centre of every reservoir engineering calculation. Moreover the rate of extraction is limited by sharply rising marginal costs. . . . However, this correction would not basically change the problem'. It should be mentioned, however, that Adelman belongs to the camp that sees no scarcity developing in the supply of minerals, which he views correctly as inventories, but believes that 'only a fraction of the minerals in the earth's crust, or in any given field, will ever be used'. (Adelman et al., 1990, p. 1). The approach I have been advocating is one that relies on a standard accountant's rule–of–thumb that estimates inventory use out of a given stock in an attempt to approximate reality. I stated in my 1981 article that factors such as the ones mentioned by Adelman et al. (1990) could be accommodated under the approach I proposed. The so–called reservoir engineering rule of always keeping a constant ratio between reserves and extraction is of dubious reliability and not essential for the calculations in any case. See El Serafy (1981).

8. See Bradford (1990). This was a comment on Maurice Scott's 'Extended Accounts for National Income and Product: A Comment' and Robert Eisner's 'Reply' to Scott in the same issue of the *Journal of Economic Literature*.

9. Ecologists tend to define substitutes more narrowly than economists who appear to favour a broad definition that allows market freedom to define what a substitute is. Pearce, Markandaya and Barbier (1989) advocated 'pairing' or 'twinning', but within a programme of many projects, rather than for each project at a time.

10. A vision of a possible course is offered in Daly and Cobb (1989). Many aspects of such a course, however, need to be much more carefully examined as the authors urge.

11. The convention of valuing GDP at factor costs and not at market prices derives from the presumption that taxes and subsidies represent deviations from genuine values produced by the market and which should provide weights for the various activities that make up the domestic product. But if a new set of environmentally inspired taxes and subsidies is viewed as necessary to correct the market's failure to put proper values on the services of natural resources, then we should regard such 'market prices' as better weights than factor costs for the purpose of estimating income in the present context.

References

ADELMAN, M. A.; DE SILVA, H; KOEHN, M.F. 1990. *User Cost in Oil Production*. Cambridge, MIT Center for Energy Policy Research. October.

BRADFORD, D. F. 1990. Comment on Scott and Eisner. *Journal of Economic Literature*, Vol. 28, No. 3., September. p. 1184.

DALY, H. E.; COBB, J.B. 1989. *For the Common Good: Redirecting the Economy Toward Community, Environment, and a Sustainable Future*. Boston, Beacon Press. 482 pp.

EL SERAFY, S. 1981. Absorptive Capacity, the Demand for Revenue and the Supply of Petroleum. *Journal of Energy and Development*. Vol. 7, No. 1. Autumn, pp. 73–88.

—. 1986. Rapporteur's Report of the October 1985 Paris Meeting. Washington, D.C., World Bank. (Mimeograph.)

—. 1991. The Environment as Capital. In R. Costanza (ed.), *Ecological Economics: The Science and Management of Sustainability*. New York, Columbia Press. 535 pp.

GELB, A. et al. 1988. *Oil Windfalls: Blessing or Curse?*. World Bank Research Publication. New York, Oxford University Press.

HICKS, J. R. 1939. *Value and Capital*, (2nd ed. 1946) Oxford, Clarendon Press. p. 187.

MCNEILL, J. 1990. Sustainable Development, Economics and the Growth Imperative. Paper presented at the Workshop on the Economics of Sustainable Development. Washington, D.C., January 1990. United States Environmental Protection Agency.

PEARCE, D.; MARKANDYA, A.; BARBIER, E. 1989. *Blueprint for a Green Economy*, London, Earthscan Publications. 192 pp.

PEZZEY, J. 1989. *Economic Analysis of Sustainable Growth and Sustainable Development, Appendix 1: Definitions of Sustainability in the Literature*. Washington, D.C., World Bank. (Environment Department Working Paper 15.)

WCED. 1987. *Our Common Future* (The Brundtland Report). Oxford, World Commission on Environment and Development, Oxford University Press. p. 43.

6

Sustainable development

The role of investment

Bernd von Droste and Peter Dogsé

Introduction

Investment, in all its different forms, shapes our lives as well as that of generations to come. Investment in education, science, technology, culture and communications, for example, continues to have crucial impacts on human welfare. In many cases, today's resource degradation is a function of earlier investment decisions about the scale and quality of consumption and production. This calls for increased understanding of investment processes for improved management of human–made and natural capital.

Rapidly increasing environmental costs prompt scientists and economists to warn that limits are being reached (see Goodland, Chapter 1), and challenges the maxim that continued economic growth leads to increased global welfare (see Tinbergen and Hueting, Chapter 4). To many observers a discussion about limits, for example to economic growth, might be seen as an academic exercise in a world where so many basic needs are still unmet. Taking these warnings seriously, however, we believe that the question has important implications, which have to be considered by development planners in all parts of the world.

That being said, this chapter is mostly directed towards the North, which is not only primarily responsible for the present situation, but has many of the resources needed to invest in development that 'meets the needs of the present without compromising the ability of future generations to meet their own needs' (WCED, 1987). Based on the relationship between environmental quality, economic performance and social welfare, it is now evident that sustainable development demands that larger investments be directed towards the environmental sector for protection and restoration of the productive and assimilative capacity of natural capital.

Increased investments will, however, not only be made for adapting to environmental limits, but also for shifting them. Investments in modern biotechnology research and production are an important example of the latter, which pose challenges with far–reaching environmental and socio–economic consequences, not the least in the South. It is by influencing today's long–term investment decisions, in areas such as biotechnology and renewable energy, that the policy and decision–making community will have the largest impact on the international community's sustainable development efforts.

Why do investments go wrong?

Policy–makers tend to underestimate the value of environmental investments for many reasons, including: time–lags (environmental costs and benefits often take time to develop but political mandates are usually short); practical difficulties in the evaluation of environmental benefits and costs; the transboundary nature of several environmental externalities making identification of national responsibilities and domestic solutions ambiguous without co–ordinated international efforts; and high discount rates (short–term time preferences). Furthermore, private investors are often discouraged to make long–term investments in natural capital due to the public–good character of such assets and the lack of property rights arrangements, making the benefits from such investments difficult to secure. Instead, they favour investments in activities generating income more quickly.

Sustainable development implies, however, that investment processes are not only understood and managed for monetary returns, but that non–monetary factors (e.g. social, cultural and ecological realities) also be considered (Young and Ishwaran, 1989). This means that the value of environmental services and goods must be estimated and incorporated in the decision–making process. The failure of traditional systems of national accounts in this respect is becoming recognized, and considerable work is being undertaken to develop accounting methods that include depreciation (as well as increases) of environmental capital assets and that subtract defensive expenditures[1] from national income (Ahmad et al., 1989; see also El Serafy, Chapter 5).

In the same way as policy– and decision–makers consult macro–economic indicators (inflation, 'growth', exchange rates and unemployment figures), they should also be provided with environmental indicators and models illustrating the state of the environment and its impact on the economy, as well as the relationship between economic activity and resource degradation. As it stands now, development models frequently ignore the direct and indirect value of natural capital, both in the economic growth process and for sustaining human welfare. Of course, the availability of such models might be limited, but enough data exist on which decisions could and should be made (Costanza, 1990).

Due to the above factors and the increased scale of human activity, there is now a long list of environmental priorities requiring large–scale investment, ranging from the atmosphere (to reduce emissions of greenhouse gases and ozone–layer–depleting chemicals), to local conservation of biological and genetic diversity. The list is so impressive that authors like Herman Daly conclude that since the productivity of human–made capital is becoming more and more constrained by the decreasing supply and quality of complementary natural capital, we are now in an era where 'investment must shift from human–made capital accumulation towards natural capital preservation and restoration' (see Daly, Chapter, 2).

Investment necessary in the short term

The economic rationality behind increased natural capital investments becomes apparent when we look at some costs and benefits involved. The world–wide lack of investment in soil protection is one practical example. Due to various short–term, income–generating activities (e.g. deforestation, intensive agriculture and irrigation) 25 billion tons of soil are lost worldwide each year. It is calculated that over a twenty–year period, a $4.5 billion/year investment in soil protection would reduce the annual cost of lost agricultural production by $26 billion (Lazarus, 1990). In addition, increased soil investments would also produce benefits outside the agricultural sector (for example, reducing sedimentation in hydro–electric dams, improving water quality and increasing fish catches).[2]

Another example is current damage to European forests from air pollution, which is conservatively estimated at $30 billion per year. Although the European countries have agreed to spend some $9 billion per year to reduce air pollution, additional investments are calculated to be cost–effective (IIASA, 1990).

In spite of the fact that today's investments are often smaller than necessary, the amount spent on mitigating environmental costs will likely fund a new industrial sector for pollution control and waste management in the near future. In the OECD countries some 9 billion tonnes of wastes were produced in 1990, including nearly 1,500 tonnes of industrial wastes (of which 300 millon tonnes were hazardous) and 420 million tonnes of municipal wastes (OECD, 1991). Estimates are that by 1992 the pollution control industry in Western Europe alone will be a $120 billion–dollar–a–year business. By 1994 more than $200 billion might have to be spent annually on clean–up and pollution control in the United States.

Increased knowledge and industrial efficiency in these fields are welcomed, but it is unfortunate that so many companies and employees will depend on continued environmental degradation for their income. The urgent need for a massively expanded waste–treatment and pollution–control sector reflects historical lack of infrastructure investments and calls for substantially increased efforts towards finding environmentally sound production processes and products.

With the increasing scarcity of natural capital goods and services, investments in the rehabilitation of degraded ecosystems have become all the more important. Not only can rehabilitated natural capital assets produce significant incomes, they often also constitute the best way to protect remaining natural areas from degradation. Since the time and investment necessary to undertake restoration activities increase significantly with the increasing level of ecosystem degradation, rapid action is essential.

Approximately 80 per cent of the potentially productive arid and semi–arid lands worldwide (representing 35 per cent of the earth's land surface) suffered from moderate to severe desertification in the early 1980s, due primarily to poor land management (Dregne, 1983). In many arid and semi–arid areas, the natural resource base is, therefore, no longer able to sustain existing human populations. Due to high population growth rates this will worsen in the near future. In the year 2000 there will be a rural population of at least 40 million in the Sahelian and Sudanese zones of West Africa (calculated from a conservative 2 per cent annual population increase). This is 3.7 million people more than what the current crop and livestock production systems of this region can support, or 19.1 million more than what can be sustained by fuel–wood, the energy source on which these societies rely (World Bank, 1985). Unless these areas are successfully rehabilitated, continued worldwide desertification may leave hundreds of millions of people as environmental refugees (Gregersen et al., 1989; Simon, 1991).

Financing investments in the South and in Eastern Europe

Although increasingly aware of environmental values but constrained by severe budgetary constraints, many developing countries find it difficult to make long-term investments in their natural capital assets, in particular since increased consumption is also seen as a major priority (African Centre for Technology Studies, 1990). Their need for additional investment resources can only be evaluated as alarming.[3] Developing countries often argue, for example, that they cannot afford environmentally sound techniques, if less expensive, but polluting alternatives exist, and that it is now their turn to benefit from the technologies the industrial world has been using for a long time.

However, as so much of today's technology is not environmentally sustainable, it is therefore not economically sustainable. As the developed world already has produced such large concentrations of environmental toxins, the value of the negative externalities that additional emissions would produce, is no longer marginal and in many cases no longer external. Developing nations therefore cannot invest in environmentally unsound techniques without facing rising domestic environmental costs, thus reducing the return on the investment and jeopardizing the success of future sustainable development. Several countries in Eastern Europe are striking examples. By pursuing economic growth at the expense of the environment they now face tremendous ecological damage. The German Institute for Economic Research has estimated that industries in Poland, the former German Democratic Republic, Czechoslovakia and the European part of the USSR will need $200 billion to reverse prior environmental neglect (Cave, 1990).

It could be argued that the developed world, by using technologies that have accumulated global toxins, to some extent has reduced the option for developing countries to use the same technologies (or any other techniques with the same impacts), because of the risk of potential future environmental catastrophes. Industrial countries should, therefore, be prepared to compensate the developed world for these closed options. This could be done partly by financing sustainable technology investments in developing countries, and partly by cutting back dramatically on their own emissions to give space for increased use of environmentally unsound technologies in developing countries without increasing the total global environmental abuse. Indeed, the North has to reduce input growth and waste, using both economic and legal instruments, while at the same time providing the South with capital and environmentally sound technologies through various arrangements, such as green–funds and debt–for–sustainable development swaps (Hansen, 1989; Dogsé and von Droste, 1990).

The Multilateral Fund agreed upon by the Contracting Parties to the Montreal Protocol to provide developing countries with additional funds for obtaining ozone-friendly technologies and replacements of CFCs, is an important achievement in this direction. The $160 million–dollar fund, will expand to $240 million if China and India — both planning major CFC production increases — eventually ratify the Montreal Protocol. This fund is now part of the $1.5 billion–dollar pilot Global Environment Facility (GEF) which is administered by the World Bank, UNEP and UNDP. GEF funds, however modest in size compared with identified needs (WRI, 1990), are to be used for investments in three additional areas: greenhouse gas emission reductions; conservation of biological and genetic diversity; and protection of international water resources.

The European Bank for Reconstruction and Development (EBRD) also has the potential to become an important funder of investments with positive environmental impact. EBRD's first loan ever, which was given to Poland for a heating project, is promising. The $50 million–dollar loan (together with a $20 million–dollar World Bank credit) aims at reducing air pollution by switching from coal to gas–fired heat generation and by promoting energy efficiency (Anon., 1991).

Developing nations cannot, however, always rely on industrial nations to develop and transfer appropriate technologies to them. Developing nations should be prepared to make part of that investment themselves so as to ensure that technologies fit their economic, cultural and natural environments. In some cases this will mean that local, small–scale, production units are stimulated, which may require that innovative finance approaches first have to be developed. Initiatives such as the Grameen Bank in Bangladesh, which in 1988 operated with 413,000 participants, has shown that it is possible to provide financial support to the rural poor and landless (World Bank, 1990). These groups, heavily dependent on the natural environment, frequently had very limited means for making long–term investment in natural capital and thus often had to sacrifice investment for consumption. Now, however, they may become vigorous promotors for sustainable resource management.

Long–term investments

By underestimating the value of our natural capital, we are now in a situation where more and more resources will have to be spent on restoration, waste disposal, and protection of the remaining natural capital, often without producing any extra gain in welfare. Although the new problems produced by modern economic growth might be soluble, the costs for doing so are unnecessarily high as many of today's environmental problems should never have been produced in the first place and their costs and the ability to solve them are very far from equally distributed. Sustainable development must, therefore, ensure that scarce resources are invested in research and in the production of processes and systems that not only avoid known problems, but also anticipate unknown costs and benefits. This requires realism and vision.

Although we are generally optimistic, the energy sector, central in all discussions on sustainable development, provides several examples of excess investment in research and development of unsustainable processes and lack of investment in renewables. One of the most glaring is the fact that in 1989 the 21 member countries of the International Energy Agency (IEA) spent 75 per cent of their $7.3 billion–dollar energy research budget on fossil fuels and nuclear energy, but only 7 per cent on renewables and 5 per cent on energy conservation (see Table 1).

The fact that investments are directed inefficiently might often depend on the institutions responsible for their administration. Institutions, which once were efficient in their field of competence and mandate, may not adapt rapidly enough to new or evolving demands. Why, for example, is there no United Nations body working on the promotion of energy conservation and renewables when there is one dedicated to the promotion of nuclear power, the International Atomic Energy Agency (IAEA)? Its 1991 budget of $179 million, with $70 million expected in additional voluntary contributions, is primarily designed to monitor nuclear proliferation, but it is also said to actively promote the export of nuclear power technology to developing nations.

Bernd von Droste and Peter Dogsé

Table 1. Energy R&D Spending by IEA governments, 1989.

Technology	Amount $ million	Share (%)
Nuclear fission	3,466	47
Fossil fuel	1,098	15
Nuclear fusion	883	12
Renewables	498	7
Conservation	367	5
Other	1,039	14
TOTAL	**7,351**	**100**

Source: Flavin and Lensen (1990).

At present developing countries get 40 per cent of their energy from renewables and less than 1 per cent from nuclear plants (Flavin and Lenssen, 1990). The creation of a United Nations agency for renewable energy sources and conservation would clearly be justified and should, therefore, be considered by UNCED.[4]

Existing institutions may reflect historical preferences rather than modern needs and the interest of 'old' organization in modern sustainability issues might be larger than their ability to cope with them. This brings up the whole issue of either establishing new institutions or up–dating existing ones — a long–term investment in itself.

Limits, research and development

The increased visibility of the costs of environmental degradation has resulted in more scientists warning that various limits are being reached, or have already been exceeded, and more economists challenge the traditional wisdom that continued economic growth leads to increased welfare (see Goodland, Chapter 1). On the question of limits, although there is scientific consensus regarding certain physical constraints and hazards to economic growth, we do not have consensus regarding our possibilities to meet these challenges or on the economic consequences of exceeding these limits — no irreversible event is, from an anthropocentric point of view, worse than our subjective, and dynamic, evaluation of it.

Doubtless humanity will also try to control future limits as has happened throughout history. This will certainly include increasingly sophisticated manipulation of biological and physical processes, ranging from micro–cosmos to the atmosphere, if not beyond. Efforts will be made to increase the photosynthetic capacities in plants by cell engineering, the rice, maize and pulse genomes might be completely mapped and genetic diseases cured, agricultural soils and oceans turned into carbon sinks (to mitigate the greenhouse effect), etc. But we must recognize that these are still unknown technologies that will probably bring unknown side effects (just as did leaded gasoline, asbestos and CFCs, etc.).

Shifting biological limits

The economic forces increasing biological productivity are already immense (see Table 2), and it would be naïve to think that major (public and private) investments will not be made for such purposes. Allocation and management of investment capital going into modern biotechnology research and production is, because of its promise, risks and socio–economic consequences, a key area of concern in sustainability discussions.[5]

Advanced knowledge about how gene expression works is now used in increased food and energy production, new medicines, raw materials and in improved environmental management. There is also great interest from the defence industry. Increased knowledge about manipulation of biological processes is, as with knowledge in general, a doubled–edged sword: the key to control is also the key to destruction. Because of the huge stakes and the vast number of actors involved in biotechnology, the whole question of moral discipline poses major concern.

Biotechnology applications can speed up or slow down entropy increases, in both unsustainable and sustainable processes, in a more equitable or less equitable international order. The particular responsibilities now facing national and international policy and decision–makers in the field of biotechnology are among the

Table 2. *Examples of commercial economic benefits from conventional crop breeding.*

Potential benefits ($ millions/year)	Commercial beneficiary	'Improvement'
4,400	Worldwide	Crossing of a perennial Mexican corn able to grow in marginal soils at high altitudes and which is resistant to seven major corn diseases with modern annual corn varieties
3,500	Asia	Improved production by incorporating dwarfism into wheat and rice
160	USA	A single gene from an Ethiopian barley plant introduced to commercial barley crops protects them from yellow dwarf virus

Source: UNEP (1990)

most urgent and difficult on their agenda.

Biotechnology is seen as a major chance for developing tropical countries to gain from their rich biological and genetic diversity. Unless developing countries become much better prepared to influence and control present and future investments in biotechnology research and production, however, they are in serious difficulty with far-reaching consequences for their economic and environmental sustainability. The risk (from a Southern perspective) is that additional comparative advantages will be given to the North making it impossible for the South to compete in the production of various agricultural goods for which there is, or will be, a large demand and high value-added potential.

By using subsidies, trade barriers and environmentally unsustainable production technologies, the North already produces agricultural surpluses that suppress world market prices and threaten production in the South. Given that the North is not prepared to forgo some of its present market control, which seriously inhibits development efforts in the South, it may not hesitate to strengthen its position further. Although perhaps not primarily as a consequence of North–South but North–North competition, the North will most likely take the lead in investing in natural capital using low–cost genetic 'raw materials' from the South. This would be analogous to human–made capital competition where the South in many cases was unable to develop competitive value–added processes (e.g. saw–mills, paper factories, metal industries etc.) and fell back on selling natural resources at falling prices.

Small farmers in developing countries may be the biggest losers in such a scenario since they are least able to undertake and influence investments needed for them to stay competitive, even on domestic markets. The socio–economic consequences of decreasing economic sustainability by the rural poor, which may force large populations to search for their livelihood in increasingly unsustainable cities, should not be underestimated. This leaves people in the South to question to what extent they actually benefit from so–called 'free–trade' and technology transfers. They must also consider what measures they eventually can take to improve their own development potential in a situation where international economic competition is so unbalanced in favour of the North.

Time for action

It will take some ten years for today's investments in research and development of new biotechnology to reap economically significant results. It will then in many cases be too late to correct for unwanted side effects and costs. The international community should therefore assess risks, benefits and costs as well as their distribution, and seek to control the development of such technology at the earliest possible stage.

Much of the discussion above points to the responsibilities of public sectors as large–scale investors. Because many large biotechnology and energy research investments are made by the private sector, however, the public sector also has the responsibility of influencing private investment.[6] Maurice Strong's statement on the importance of incorporating the private sector into development planning is particularly relevant: 'Business is the major engine of development in our society. And, therefore if we can't influence business, we really can't influence development' (Dampier, 1982). In particular this will mean taking the needs of the South into consideration, including elaboration and assessment of how, through legal, economic and policy arrangements, developing countries can best be strengthened in their research and investment capacities.

Conclusion

Compared with the costs, 0.8 to 1.5 per cent of GDP, industrial countries have received significant benefits from their environmental programmes during the last twenty years (OECD, 1991). Although natural capital investments made are too low, for those countries who have invested even less, or hope to avoid such investments in the future, the bill will get much higher.

It is, therefore, encouraging to note that public opinion in the United States, Japan and fourteen European countries now indicates strong support for the environment, even in situations where protection of the environment would reduce economic growth (OECD, 1991). Such attitudes are a good basis for the institutional changes in the industrial world needed for improved understanding and management of investment capital in relation to existing (and possibly shifted) ecological constraints to economic growth. It is also the best guarantee that innovative financial bodies, such as GEF, will get increased resources and mandates to help promote sustainable investment practices in the South. UNCED'92 is, of course, an opportunity of utmost importance to bring about such changes.

However, throughout history, despite being aware of environmental constraints, societies failed to secure a sustainable balance between immediate consumption and long–term natural capital investment and, therefore, eventually collapsed (Ponting, 1990). Furthermore, although these societies were constrained by only local or regional environmental limits, today's global limits will require a level of international co–ordination and co–operation never before necessary in the history of humanity.

■

Acknowledgements

The authors are indebted to Robert Goodland, Ignacy Sachs and Dana Silk for valuable comments on an earlier version of this chapter.

Notes

1. Costs necessary to maintain (defend) a certain level of welfare that threatens to fall because of unwanted side–effects of consumption and production, such as pollution.

2. It has been estimated that siltation of dams feeding hydropower turbines involves a loss of some 148,000 gigawatt hours, which at $15 per barrel would cost some $4 billion per year to replace using oil–fired thermal generation (Pearce, 1987).

3. The World Resources Institute (WRI) has estimated that the Third World's unmet financial needs for maintaining their natural resources as 'the basis for meeting the needs for current and future generations' amounts to $20–50 billion per year over the next decade (WRI, 1990).

4. The UNEP Collaborating Centre on Energy and Environment linked to the Risoe National Laboratory in Denmark, which was opened on 1 October 1990, may be a good starting point towards this end.

5. Biotechnology has been defined as 'the application of biological systems and organisms to scientific, industrial, agricultural, health and environment processes and uses'. 'Organisms' includes animals, plants and microbes. 'New' biotechnology refers to the use of cell fusion, cell and tissue culture, recombinant DNA and novel bioprocessing methods. 'Old' or classical biotechnology means the use of microbes for baking, brewing, or other fermentation processes, or selective breeding in agriculture and animal husbandry (Giddings and Persley, 1990).

6. In 1987, total research and development investment in agricultural biotechnology was estimated at $900 million, of which more than 60 per cent was in the private sector (Giddings and Persley, 1990).

References

AFRICAN CENTRE FOR TECHNOLOGY STUDIES. 1990. *The Nairobi Declaration on Climatic Change. International Conference on Global Warming and Climate Change: African Perspectives.* Nairobi, African Centre for Technology Studies. May 2–4.

AHMAD, Y. J.; EL SERAFY, S.; LUTZ, E. (eds.). 1989. *Environment Accounting for Sustainable Development.* Washington, D.C., World Bank. 100 pp.

ANON. 1991. European Development Bank Makes First Loan. *International Herald Tribune,* 22 June, p. 13.

CAVE, S. 1990. Cleaning up Eastern Europe. *Our Planet,* Vol. 2, No. 2., pp. 4–7. New York, United Nations Environment Programme.

COSTANZA, R. 1990. Ecological Economics as a Framework for Developing Sustainable National Policies. In: B. Aniansson; U. Svedin, (eds.), *Towards an Ecological Sustainable Economy.* Report from a Policy Seminar held in Stockholm, Sweden, 3–4 January 1990, arranged by the Swedish Council for Planning and Coordination of Research (FRN) on behalf of the Environmental Advisory Council of the Swedish Government. Stockholm. 144 pp. (FRN Rapport, 90:6.)

DAMPIER, W. 1982. Strong Assesses the Decade Since Stockholm. In: Synopsis: Ten Years After Stockholm: A Decade of Environmental Debate. *Ambio,* Vol. 11, No. 4., pp. 229–31.

DOGSÉ, P.; VON DROSTE, B. 1990. *Debt–for–Nature Exchanges and Biosphere Reserves: Experiences and Potential.* MAB Digest, No. 6. Paris, UNESCO. 88 pp.

DREGNE, H. E. 1983. Desertification of Arid Lands. *Advances in Desert and Arid Land Technology and Development,* Vol. 3. New York, Harwood Academic Publishers. 242 pp.

FLAVIN, C.; LENSEN, N. 1990. *Beyond the Petroleum Age: Designing a Solar Economy,* Washington, D.C., Worldwatch Institute. (Worldwatch Paper 100.)

GIDDINGS, L. V.; PERSLEY, G. 1990. Biotechnology and Biodiversity. Study prepared for United Nations Environment Programme, 12 October. (UNEP/Bio.Div./SWGB. 1/3.)

GREGERSEN, H.; DRAPER, S.; ELZ, D. (eds.). 1989. *People and Trees: The Role of Social Forestry in Sustainable Development.* Washington, D.C., World Bank. 273 pp.

HANSEN, S. 1989. Debt for Nature Swaps — Overview and Discussion of Key Issues. *Ecological Economics,* Vol. 1, No. 1., pp. 77–93.

IIASA. 1990. Comprehensive Study of European Forests Assesses Damage and Economic Lossesfrom Air Pollution. *News Release,* No. 5, December. IIASA, International Institute for Applied Systems Analysis.

LAZARUS, D. S. 1990. Save our Soils. *Our Planet*, Vol. 2, No. 4., New York, United Nations Environment Programme.

OECD (Organisation for Economic Co–operation and Development). 1991. *The State of the Environment*. Paris, OECD.

PEARCE, D. 1987. Economic Values and the Natural Environment. *University College London Discussion Papers in Economics*, Vol. 87, No. 8., pp. 1–20.

PONTING, C. 1990. Historical Perspectives on Sustainable Development. *Environment*, Vol. 32, No. 9.

SIMON, B. 1991. Report Predicts Flood of 'Environmental Refugees'. *Financial Times*, 25 June, p. 6.

UNEP (United Nations Environment Programme). 1990. Note by UNEP on Basic Issues With Respect to Biotechnology and Conservation of Biological Diversity. Ad hoc Working Group of Experts on Biological Diversity, Subworking Group on Biotechnology. Nairobi, UNEP, 14–16 November, 1990. (UNEP/Bio.Div./SWGB.1/2, 15 October, 1990, Annex 2.)

WORLD BANK. 1985. *Desertification in Sahelian and Sudanian Zones in West Africa*. Washington, D.C., World Bank, 60 pp.

—. 1990. *World Development Report 1990*. Washington, D.C., World Bank. 67 pp.

WRI (World Resources Institute). 1990. *Natural Endowments: Financing Resource Conservation for Development*. Washington, D.C., WRI. 33 pp.

7

The ecological economics of sustainability

Investing in natural capital

Robert Costanza

An ecological economic world–view

To achieve global sustainability, we need to stop thinking of ecological and economic goals as being in conflict. Economic systems are dependent on their ecological life–support systems and we must realize that fact and incorporate it into our thinking and actions at a very basic level if we are to sustain our global household. A house divided against itself cannot stand.

To achieve sustainability we must develop an *ecological economics* that goes well beyond the conventional disciplines of ecology and economics to a truly integrative synthesis (Costanza, 1991).

Figure 1 illustrates one aspect of the relationship between ecological economics and the conventional approaches; the domains of the different subdisciplines. The upper left box represents the domain of 'conventional' economics, the interactions of economic sectors (like mining, manufacturing, or households) with each other. The domain of 'conventional' ecology is the lower right box, the interactions of ecosystems and their components with each other. The lower left box represents the inputs from ecological to economic sectors. This is the usual domain of *resource* economics and environmental impact analysis: the use of renewable and non–renewable natural resources by the economy. The upper right box represents the 'use' by ecological sectors of economic 'products'. The products of interest in this box are usually unwanted by–products of production and the ultimate wastes from consumption. This is the usual domain of *environmental* economics and environmental impact analysis: pollution and its mitigation, prevention and mediation. Ecological economics encompasses and transcends these disciplinary boundaries. Ecological economics sees the human economy as part of a larger whole. Its domain is the entire web of interactions between economic and ecological sectors.

Table 1 presents some of the other major differences between ecological economics (EE) and conventional economics (CEcon) and conventional ecology (CEcol). The basic world view of CEcon is one in which individual human consumers are the central figures. Their tastes and preferences are taken as given and are the dominant, determining force. The resource base is viewed as essentially limitless due to technical progress and infinite substitutability. EE takes a more holistic view with humans as one component (albeit a very important one) in the overall system. Human preferences, understanding, technology and cultural organization all co–evolve to reflect broad ecological opportunities and constraints. Humans have a special place in the system because they are responsible for understanding their own role in the larger system and managing it for sustainability. This basic world–view is similar to that of CEcol, in which the resource base is limited and humans are just another (albeit seldom studied) species. But EE differs

from CEcol in the importance it gives to humans as a species, and its emphasis on the mutual importance of cultural and biological evolution.

We must acknowledge that the human system is a subsystem within the larger ecological system. This implies not only a relationship of interdependence, but ultimately a relation of dependence of the subsystem on the larger parent system. The first questions to ask about a subsystem are: How big is it relative to the total system, how big can it be, and how big should it be? These questions of scale are only now beginning to be asked (Daly and Cobb, 1989).

The presumed goals of the systems under study are also quite distinct, especially at the macro–level. The macro–goal

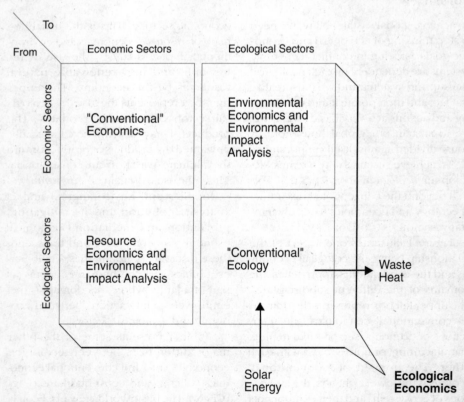

*Figure 1: **The domains of conventional economics, conventional ecology, environmental and resource economics, and ecological economics.***

of EE is sustainability of the combined ecological economic system. CEcol's macro–goal of species survival is similar to sustainability, but is generally confined to single species and not the whole system. CEcon emphasizes growth rather than sustainability at the macro–level . At the micro–level, EE is unique in acknowledging the two–way linkages between scales, rather than the one–way view of the conventional sciences in which all macro behaviour is the simple aggregation of micro behaviour. In EE, social organization and cultural institutions at higher levels of the space/time hierarchy ameliorate conflicts produced by myopic pursuit of micro goals at lower levels, and vise versa.

Perhaps the key distinctions between EE and the conventional sciences lie in their academic stances, and their assumptions about technical progress. As already noted, EE is transdisciplinary, pluralistic, integrative, and more focused on problems than on tools.

CEcon is very optimistic about the ability of technology ultimately to remove all resource constraints to continued economic growth. CEcol really has very little to say directly about technology, since it tends to ignore humans altogether. But to the extent that it has an opinion, it would be pessimistic about technology's ability to remove resource constraints because all other existing natural ecosystems that do not include humans are observed to be resource limited. EE is prudently sceptical in this regard. Given our high level of un certainty about this issue, it is irrational to bank on technology's ability to remove resource constraints. If we guess wrong then the result will be disastrous — an ir reversible destruction of our resource base and civilization itself. We should at least for the time being assume that technology will not be able to remove resource constraints. If it does we can be pleasantly surprised. If it does

not we are still left with a sustainable system. EE assumes this prudently sceptical stance on technical progress.

Sustainability: maintaining our global life support–system

While acknowledging that the sustainability concept requires much additional research, we can offer the following working definition: Sustainability is a relationship between dynamic human economic systems and larger dynamic, but normally slower–changing ecological systems, in which: (a) human life can continue indefinitely; (b) human individuals can flourish, (c) human cultures can develop; but in which (d) effects of human activities remain within bounds, so as not to destroy the diversity, complexity, and function of the ecological life support system.

'Sustainability' does not imply a static, much less a stagnant economy, but we must be careful to distinguish between 'growth' and 'development', as specified above. Economic growth, which is an increase in quantity, cannot be sustainable indefinitely on a finite planet. Economic development, which is an improvement in the quality of life without necessarily causing an increase in quantity of resources consumed, may be sustainable. Sustainable growth is an impossibility. Sustainable development must become our primary long–term policy goal.

The most obvious danger of ignoring the role of nature in economics is that nature is the economy's life–support system, and by ignoring it we may inadvertently damage it beyond it's ability to repair itself. Indeed, there is much evidence that we have already done so (see Goodland, Chapter 1). Current economic systems do not *inherently* incorporate any concern about the sustainability of our natural life–support system and the economies which depend on it (Costanza and Daly, 1987).

Table 1: *Comparison of "conventional" economics and ecology with ecological economics.*

	"Conventional" Economics	"Conventional" Ecology	Ecological Economics
Basic World View	Mechanistic, Static, Atomistic Individual tastes and preferences taken as given and the dominant force. The resource base viewed as essentially limitless due to technical progress and infinite substitutability	Evolutionary, Atomistic Evolution acting at the genetic level viewed as the dominant force. The resource base is limited. Humans are just another species but are rarely studied	Dynamic, Systems, Evolutionary Human preferences, understanding, technology and organisation co-evolve to reflect broad ecological opportunities and constraints. Humans are responsible for understanding their role in the larger system and managing it for sustainability.
Time Frame	Short 50 years maximum, 1-4 years usual	Multi-Scale Days to eons, but time scales often define non-communicating sub-disciplines	Multi-scale Days to eons, multiscale synthesis
Space Frame	Local to international Framework invarient at increasing spatial scale, basic units change from individuals to firms to countries	Local to regional Most research has focused on relatively small research sites in single ecosystems, but larger scales becoming more important recently	Local to global Hierarchy of scales
Species Frame	Humans only Plants and animals only rarely included for contributary value	Non-Humans only Attempts to find "pristine" ecosystems untouched by humans	Whole ecosystem including humans Acknowledges interconnections between humans and rest of nature
Primary Macro goal	Growth of national economy	Survival of Species	Sustainability of ecological economic system
Primary Micro goal	Max. profits (firms) Max. utility (individuals) All agents following micro goals leads to macro goal being fulfilled. External costs and benefits given lip service but usually ignored	Maximum reproductive sucess All agents following micro goals leads to macro goal being fulfilled	Must be adjusted to reflect system goals Social organization and cultural institutions at higher levels of the space/time hierarchy ameliorate conflicts produced by myopic pursuit of micro goals at lower levels, and vice versa
Assumptions about technical progress	Very optimistic	Pessimistic or no opinion	Prudently skeptical
Academic stance	Disciplinary Monistic, focus on mathematical tools	Disciplinary More pluralistic than economics, but still focused on tools and techniques. Few rewards for comprehensive, integrative work.	Transdisciplinary pluralistic, focus on problems

In an important sense, sustainability is merely justice with respect to future generations. This includes future generations of other species, even though our main interest may be in our own species.

Sustainability has been variously construed (see Pezzey 1989; WCED, 1987) but a useful definition is the amount of consumption that can be continued indefinitely without degrading capital stocks — including 'natural capital' stocks. In a business, capital stock includes long–term assets such as buildings and machinery that serve as the means of production. Natural capital is the soil and atmospheric structure, plant and animal biomass, etc., that, taken together, forms the basis of all ecosystems. This natural capital stock uses primary inputs (sunlight) to produce the range of ecosystem services and physical natural resource flows. Examples of natural capital include forests, fish populations and petroleum deposits. The natural resource flows yielded by these natural capital stocks are, respectively, cut timber, caught fish, and pumped crude oil.

We have now entered a new era in which the limiting factor in development is no longer human–made capital but remaining natural capital. Timber is limited by remaining forests, not saw–mill capacity; fish catch is limited by fish populations, not by fishing boats; crude oil is limited by remaining petroleum deposits, not by pumping and drilling capacity. Most economists view natural and human–made capital as substitutes rather than complements. Consequently neither factor can be limiting. Only if factors are complementary can one be limiting. Ecological economists see human–made and natural capital as fundamentally complementary and therefore emphasize the importance of limiting factors and changes in the pattern of scarcity. This is a fundamental difference that needs to be reconciled.

To implement sustainability, all projects should meet the following criteria. For renewable resources, the rate of harvest should not exceed the rate of regeneration (sustainable yield) and the rates of waste generation from projects should not exceed the assimilative capacity of the environment (sustainable waste disposal). For non–renewable resources, the rates of waste generation from projects shall not exceed the assimilative capacity of the environment and the depletion of the non–renewable resources should require comparable development of renewable substitutes for that resource. These are safe, minimum sustainability standards; and once met, projects should be selected that have the highest rates of return based on other, more traditional economic criteria.

Maintaining and investing in natural capital to ensure sustainability

A minimum necessary condition for sustainability is the maintenance of the total natural capital stock at or above the current level. While a lower stock of natural capital may be sustainable, given our uncertainty and the dire consequences of guessing wrong, it is best to at least provisionally assume that we are at or below the range of sustainable stock levels and allow no further decline in natural capital. This 'constancy of total natural capital' rule can thus be seen as a prudent minimum condition for ensuring sustainability, to be abandoned only when solid evidence to the contrary can be offered. In fact, we should begin the process of reinvesting in natural capital stocks to bring them back to safe minimum standards.

There is disagreement between technological optimists (who see technical progress eliminating all resource constraints to growth and development) and technological sceptics (who do not see as much scope for this approach and fear irreversible use of resources and damage to natural capital). By limiting total system natural capital at current levels (preferably by using higher severance and consumption taxes) we can satisfy both the sceptics (as resources will be conserved for future generations) and the optimists (as this will raise the price of natural capital resources and more rapidly induce the technical change they predict). By limiting physical growth, only development is allowed and this may proceed without endangering sustainability.

Policy instruments: environmental insurance bonds

We need to explore promising alternatives to our current command and control environmental management systems, and to modify existing government agencies and other institutions accordingly. The enormous uncertainty about local and transnational environmental impacts needs to be incorporated into decision–making. We also need to better understand the sociological, cultural, and political criteria for acceptance or rejection of policy instruments.

One example of an innovative policy instrument currently being studied is a flexible environmental insurance system designed to incorporate environmental criteria and uncertainty into the market system, and to induce positive environmental technological innovation (Perrings, 1989; Costanza and Perrings, 1990).

In addition to direct charges for known environmental damages, a company would be required to post an insurance bond equal to the current best estimate of the largest potential future environmental damages; the money would be kept in interest–bearing escrow accounts.

After the project, the bond (plus a portion of the interest) would be returned if the firm could show that the suspected damages had not occurred or would not occur. If they did, the bond would be used to rehabilitate or repair the environment and to compensate injured parties. Thus, the burden of proof would be shifted from the public to the resource–user and a strong economic incentive would be provided to research the true costs of environmentally damaging activities and to develop cost–effective pollution control technologies. This is an extension of the 'polluter pays' principle to 'the polluter pays for uncertainty as well'. Other innovative policy instruments include tradeable pollution and depletion quotas at both national and international levels. Also worthy of mention is the new Global Environment Facility of the World Bank, which will provide concessionary funds for investments that reduce global externalities.

Economic incentives: linking revenues and uses

We should implement fees on the destructive use of natural capital to promote more efficient use, and ease up on income taxes, especially on low incomes in the interest of equity. Fees, taxes and subsidies should be used to change the prices of activities that interfere with sustainability relative to those that are compatible with it. This can be accomplished by using the funds generated to support an alternative to undesirable activities that are being taxed. For example a tax on all greenhouse gases, with the size of the tax linked to the impact of each gas, could be linked to development of alternatives to fossil fuel. Petrol tax revenues could be used to support public transport and cycle lanes.

Current policies that subsidize environmentally harmful activities should be stopped. For example, subsidies on virgin material extraction should be stopped. This will also allow recycling options to compete effectively. Crop subsidies that dramatically increase pesticide and fertilizer use should be eliminated, and forms of positive incentives should also be used. For example, debt for nature swaps should be supported and receive much more funding. We should also offer prestigious prizes for work that increases awareness of, or contributes to, sustainability issues, such as changes in behaviour that develop a culture of maintenance (i.e. cars that last for fifty years) or promotes capital and resource saving improvements (i.e. affordable, efficient housing and water supplies).

Ecological economics research

While economics has developed many useful tools of analysis, it has not directed these tools toward the thorny questions that arise when considering the concept and implementation of sustainability. In particular, we need a better understanding of preference formation, especially time preference formation. We also need to understand how individual time preferences and group time preferences may differ, and how the preferences of institutions that will be critical to the success or failure of sustainability are established. Up to now, we have paid too little attention to ecological feedbacks. An understanding of these will be critical for the implementation of sustainability goals. We need to concentrate on the valuation of important non–market goods and services provided by ecosystems (Costanza et al., 1989).

Ecological economics education

We need to develop an ecological economics core curriculum and degree granting programmes that embody the skills of both economics and ecology. This implies a curriculum with some blending of physical, chemical and biological sciences, and economics. Within this curriculum quantitative methods are essential, but they should be problem–directed rather than just mathematical tools for their own sake. Experimentation capacity is needed to provide ecological economics with a solid empirical base built upon creative and comprehensive theory. We need to develop extension programmes that can effectively transfer information among both disciplines and nations.

Institutional changes

Institutions with the flexibility necessary to deal with ecologically sustainable development are lacking. Indeed many financial institutions are built on the assumption of continuous exponential growth and will face major restructuring in a sustainable economy. Many existing institutions have fragmented mandates and policies, and often have not optimally used market and non–market forces to resolve environmental problems. They have also conducted inadequate benefit/cost analyses by not incorporating ecological costs; used short–term planning horizons; inappropriately assigned property rights (public and private) to resources; and not made appropriate use of incentives.

There is a lack of awareness and education about sustainability, the environment, and causes of environmental degradation. In addition, much environmental knowledge held by indigenous peoples is being lost, including knowledge of species, particularly in the tropics. Institutions have been slow to respond to new information and shifts in values, for example threats to biodiversity or rapid changes in communications technologies. Finally, many institutions do not freely share or disseminate information; do not provide public access to decision–making; and do not devote serious attention to determining and representing the wishes of their constituencies.

Many of these problems are a result of the inflexible bureaucratic structure of many modern institutions. Experience (e.g. Japanese industry) has shown that less bureaucratic, more flexible, more peer–to–peer institutional structures can be much more efficient and effective. We need to de–bureaucratize institutions so that they can effectively respond to the coming challenges of achieving sustainability. ∎

References

COSTANZA, R. (ed.). 1991. *Ecological Economics: The Science and Management of Sustainability.* New York, Columbia University Press. 435 pp.

COSTANZA, R.; DALY, H.E. 1987. Toward an Ecological Economics. *Ecological Modeling,* Vol. 38, pp. 1–7.

COSTANZA, R.; FARBER, S.C.; MAXWELL, J. 1989. The Valuation and Management of Wetland Ecosystems. *Ecological Economics,* Vol. 1, pp. 335–61.

COSTANZA, R.; PERRINGS, C.H. 1990. A Flexible Assurance Bonding System for Improved Environmental Management. *Ecological Economics,* Vol. 2, pp. 57–76.

DALY, H. E.; COBB, J.B. 1989. *For the Common Good: Redirecting the Economy Toward Community, the Environment, and a Sustainable Future.* Boston, Beacon Press. 482 pp.

PERRINGS, C. H. 1989. Environmental Bonds and the Incentive to Research in Activities Involving Uncertain Future Effects. *Ecological Economics,* Vol. 1, pp. 95–110.

PEZZEY, J. 1989. Economic Analysis of Sustainable Growth and Sustainable Development. Washington, D.C., World Bank. (Environment Department Working Paper, 15.)

WCED, 1987. *Our Common Future.* (The Brundtland Report). Oxford, World Commission on Environment and Development/Oxford University Press. 387 pp.

8

From growth to sustainable development[1]

Lester R. Brown, Sandra Postel and Christopher Flavin

Introduction

For much of this century, economic debate has focused on whether capitalism or socialism is the best way to organize a modern industrial economy. That argument now seems to be over, as the countries of Eastern Europe move swiftly towards market mechanisms and the Soviet economy teeters on the brink of collapse. Yet even before the political dust from these transformations settles, a new, more fundamental question has arisen: How can we design a vibrant economy that does not destroy the natural resources and environmental systems on which it depends?

The vast scale and rapid growth of the 20,000–billion–dollar global economy are hailed as great achievements of our time. But as the pace of environmental deterioration quickens, the consequences of failing to bridge the gap between the workings of economic systems and natural ones are becoming all too clear. [2]

Redirecting the global economy towards environmental sustainability requires fundamental reforms at both the international and national levels. In an age when tropical deforestation in one country reduces the entire earth's biological wealth, when chemicals released on one continent can lead to skin cancer on another, and when CO_2 emissions anywhere hasten climate change everywhere, economic policy–making is no longer exclusively a national concern.

Greatly lessening the developing world's debt burden is a prerequisite for an environmentally sustainable world economy. By 1989, the Third World's external debt stood at $1,200 billion, 44 per cent of its collective GNP. In some countries, the figure was far higher — 140 per cent in Egypt and Zaire, and a staggering 400 per cent in Mozambique. Developing countries paid $77 billion in interest on their debts that year, and repaid 85 billion dollar's worth of principal. Since the mid 1980s, the traditional flow of capital from the developed to the developing world has been increasingly offset by a flow of interest and dividends in the opposite direction. Preliminary data for all flows, including grants, show an outflow from the developing countries of $2.7 billion in 1989, which compares with an inflow of $51 billion in 1981 (World Bank,

1989; OECD, 1990 *a*).

Lack of capital has made it nearly impossible for developing countries to invest adequately in forest protection, soil conservation, irrigation improvements, more energy–efficient technologies, or pollution control devices. Even worse, growing debts have compelled them to sell off natural resources, often their only source of foreign currency. Like a consumer forced to pawn the family heirlooms to pay off credit–card bills, developing countries are plundering forests, decimating fisheries, and depleting water supplies — regardless of the long–term consequences. Unfortunately, no global pawnbroker is holding on to this inheritance until the world can afford to buy it back.

Reforming foreign assistance is also critical. Very little of the aid money disbursed to developing countries by governments and international lending institutions supports ecologically sound development. The World Bank, the largest single funder, lacks a coherent vision of a sustainable economy, and thus its lending priorities often run counter to the goal of creating one. Bilateral aid agencies, with a few important exceptions, do little better. Moreover, the scale of total lending falls far short of that needed to help the Third World escape from the overlapping traps of poverty, overpopulation, and ecological decline.

Instruments of economic reform

At the heart of the dilemma at the national level is the failure of economies to incorporate environmental costs into private decisions, which results in society at large bearing them, often in unanticipated ways. Automobile drivers do not pay the full costs of local air pollution or long–term climate change when they fill their gas tanks, nor do farmers pick up the whole tab for the health and ecological risks of using pesticides.

Many industrial nations now spend 1–2 per cent of their total economic output on pollution control, and these figures will increase in the years ahead. Such large sums spent on capturing pollutants at the end of the pipe, while necessary, are to some extent a measure of the economy's failure to foster practices that curb pollution at its source. Governments mandate catalytic converters for cars, but neglect energy–efficient transport systems that would lessen automobile dependence. They require expensive methods of treating hazardous waste, while doing little to encourage industries to reduce their generation of waste (OECD, 1990*b*; Farber and Rutlege, 1990).

Of the many tools governments can use to reorient economic behaviour, fiscal policies offer some of the most powerful. In particular, partially replacing income taxes with environmental taxes could greatly speed the transition to an environmentally sustainable economy without necessarily increasing the total tax burden. Designed to make prices better reflect true costs, a comprehensive set of environmental taxes would include, for example, levies on carbon emissions from fossil fuels, hazardous waste, paper produced from virgin pulp, pesticide sales, and ground-water depletion. Shifting the tax base in this way would help ensure that those causing environmental harm pay the price, rather than society as a whole, and thereby encourage more environmentally sound practices.

A question of scale

Even if debt is relieved, development aid is restructured, and an array of green taxes are instituted, there remains the vexing problem of the economy's scale. Listening to most economists and politicians, unlimited expansion of the economy seems not only possible but desirable. Political leaders tout growth as the answer to unemployment, poverty, ailing industries, fiscal crises and myriad other societal ills. To question the wisdom of growth seems almost blasphemous, so ingrained is it in popular thinking about how the world works.

Yet to agree that creating an environmentally sustainable economy is necessary is to acknowledge that limits on some forms of growth are inevitable — in particular the consumption of physical resources. Textbook models often portray the economy as a self–contained system, with money flowing between consumers and businesses in a closed loop. In reality, however, the economy is not isolated. It operates within the boundaries of a global ecosystem with finite capacities to produce fresh water, form new topsoil and absorb pollution. As a subset of the biosphere, the economy cannot outgrow its physical limits and still remain intact (see Daly, 1990; Ehrlich, 1989).

With an annual output of $20,000 billion, the global economy now produces in seventeen days what it took an entire year to generate in 1900. Already , economic activity has breached numerous local, regional, and global thresholds, resulting in the spread of deserts, acidification of lakes and forests, and the build–up of greenhouse gases. If growth proceeds along the lines of recent decades, it is only a matter of time before global systems collapse under the pres-sure. [3]

One useful measure of the economy's size relative to the earth's life–supporting capacity is the share of the planet's photosynthetic product now devoted to human activity. 'Net primary production' is the amount of solar energy fixed by green plants through photosynthesis minus the energy used by those plants themselves. It is, in essence, the planet's total food resource, the biochemical energy that supports all forms of animal life, from earthworms to humans.

Vitousek and his colleagues estimate that 40 per cent of the earth's annual net primary production on land now goes directly to meet human needs or is indirectly used or destroyed by human activity — leaving 60 percent for the millions of other land–based species with which humans share the planet. While it took all of human history to reach this point, the share could double to 80 per cent by 2030 if current rates of population growth and consumption continue; rising per capita consumption could shorten the doubling time considerably. Along the way, with people usurping an ever larger share of the earth's life–sustaining energy, natural systems will unravel faster. Exactly when vital thresholds will be crossed irreversibly is impossible to say. But as Vitousek and his colleagues state, those 'who believe that limits to growth are so distant as to be of no consequence for today's decision makers appear unaware of these biological realities.' (Vitousek et al., 1986; PRB, 1990).

Toward greater efficiency and equity

For humanity to avoid the wholesale breakdown of natural systems requires not just a slowing in the expansion of our numbers but a shift from the pursuit of growth to that of sustainable progress — human betterment that does not come at the expense of future generations. The first and easiest phase in the transition is to increase greatly the efficiency with which water, energy, and materials are used, which will allow people's needs to be satisfied with fewer resources and less environmental harm. This shift is already under way, but is proceeding at a glacial pace compared with what is needed.

One example of the necessary approach is in California. Pioneering energy policies there have fostered utility investments in efficiency, causing electricity use per person to decline 0.3 per cent between 1978 and 1988, compared with an 11 per cent increase in the rest of the United States. Californians suffered no drop in living standards as a result; indeed, their overall welfare improved since their electricity bills were reduced and their cooking, lighting and other electrical needs were met with less sacrifice of air quality (United States Department of Energy, 1988, 1990).

Producing goods and services as efficiently as possible and with the most environmentally benign technologies available will move societies a long way toward sustainability, but it will not allow them to achieve it. Continuing growth in material consumption — the number of cars and air–conditioners, the amount of paper used, and the like — will eventually overwhelm gains from efficiency, causing total resource use (and all the corresponding environmental damage) to rise. A halving of pollution emissions from individual cars, for example, will not result in much improvement in air quality if the total distance driven doubles, as it has in the United States since 1965.[4]

This aspect of the transition from growth to sustainability is thus far more difficult, as it goes to the heart of people's consumption patterns. In poorer countries, simply meeting the basic needs of growing human numbers will require that consumption of water, energy and forest products increases, even if these resources are used with the utmost efficiency. But the wealthier industrial countries — especially the dozen that have stabilized their population size, including Austria, Germany, Italy, Norway, Sweden, and Switzerland — are in the best position to begin satisfying their needs with no net degradation of the natural resource base (PRB, 1990). These countries could be the first to benefit from realizing that some growth costs more than it is worth, and that an economy's optimum size is not its maximum size.

Quality over quantity

GNP becomes an obsolete measure of progress in a society striving to meet people's needs as efficiently as possible and with the least damage to the environment. What counts is not growth in output, but the quality of services rendered. Bicycles and light rail, for instance, are less resource–intensive forms of transportation than automobiles are, and contribute less to GNP. But a shift to mass transit and cycling for most passenger trips would enhance urban life by eliminating traffic jams, reducing smog and making cities safer for pedestrians. GNP would go down, but overall well–being would increase (see Anderson, 1989; Daly and Cobb, 1989).

Likewise, investing in water–efficient appliances and irrigation systems instead of building more dams and diversion canals would meet water needs with less harm to the environment. Since massive water projects consume more resources than efficiency investments do, GNP would tend to decline. But quality of life would improve. It becomes clear that striving to boost GNP is often inappropriate and counterproductive. As ecologist and philosopher Garrett Hardin puts it: 'For a statesman to try to maximize the GNP is about as sensible as for a composer of music to try to maximize the number of notes in a symphony.' (Hardin, 1990).

Abandoning growth as an overriding goal does not and must not mean forsaking the poor. Rising incomes and material consumption are essential to improving well–being in much of the Third World. But contrary to what political leaders imply, global economic growth as currently measured is not the solution to poverty. Despite the fivefold rise in world economic output since 1950, 1.2 billion people — more than ever before — live in absolute poverty today. More growth of the sort engineered in recent decades will not save the poor; only strategies to distribute income and wealth more equitably can do so (Durning, 1989).

A higher social order

Formidable barriers stand in the way of shifting from growth to real progress as the central goal of economic policy. The vision that growth conjures up of an expanding pie of riches is a powerful and convenient political tool because it allows the tough issues of income inequality and skewed wealth distribution to be avoided. As long as there is growth, there is hope that the lives of the poor can be bettered without sacrifices from the rich. The reality, however, is that achieving an environmentally sustainable global economy is not possible without the fortunate limiting their consumption in order to leave room for the poor to increase theirs.

With the ending of the Cold War and the fading of ideological barriers, an opportunity has opened to build a new world upon the foundations of peace. A sustainable economy represents nothing less than a higher social order — one as concerned with future generations as with our own, and more focused on the health of the planet and the poor than on material acquisitions and military might. Although it is a fundamentally new endeavour, with many uncertainties, it is far less risky than continuing with business as usual. ∎

Notes

1. Based on L.R. Brown et al., *State of the World 1991*. New York, W. W. Norton, 1991.

2. The 20,000 billion dollar world economy is a Worldwatch Institute estimate based on 1988 gross world product from the Central Intelligence Agency (CIA, 1989*a*), with Soviet and Eastern Europe on gross national products extrapolated from Paul Marer (1985), and with adjustment to 1990 based on growth rates from IMF (1990), and CIA (1989*b*).

3. 1900 Global World Output, from Brown and Postel (1987).

4. Total vehicle kilometres for 1965–70 from United States Department of Commerce (1975), for 1970–88 from United States Department of Energy (1988).

References

ANDERSON, H. 1989. Moving Beyond Economism: New Indicators for Culturally Specific, Sustainable Development. *Redefining Wealth and Progress: New Ways to Measure Economic, Social and Environmental Change.* New York, Bootstrap Press. (Caracas Report on Alternative Development Indicators.)

BROWN, L. R.; POSTEL, S. 1987. Thresholds of Change. In: L.R. Brown et al., (eds), *State of the World 1987.* Washington, D.C., W. W. Norton.

CIA (Central Intelligence Agency). 1989*a*. *Handbook of Economic Statistics 1989.* Washington, D.C., CIA.

—. 1989*b*. *Handbook of Economic Tables, Budget of the United States Government, Fiscal Year 1990*. Washington, D.C., CIA.

DALY, H. E. 1990. Towards an Environmental Macroeconomics. Paper presented at the conference on The Ecological Economics of Sustainability: Making Local and Short Term Goals Consistent with Global and Long Term Goals, held at the International Society for Ecological Economics, Washington, D.C., May 1990.

DALY, H. E.; COBB, J.R. 1989. *For the Common Good: Redirecting the Economy Toward Community, the Environment, and a Sustainable Future*. Boston, Beacon Press. 482 pp.

DURNING, A. 1989. *Poverty and The Environment: Reversing the Downward Spiral*. Washington, D.C., Worldwatch Institute.

EHRLICH, P. R. 1989. The Limits to Substitution: Meta–Resource Depletion and a New Economic–Ecological Paradigm. *Ecological Economics*, Vol. 1, No. 1, pp. 9–16.

FARBER, K. D.; RUTLEGE, G.L. 1990. Pollution Abatement and Control Expenditures, 1984–87. *Survey of Current Business*. Washington, D.C., United States Department of Commerce.

HARDIN, G. 1990. Paramount Positions in Ecological Economics. Paper presented at the conference on The Ecological Economics of Sustainability: Making Local and Short Term Goals Consistent with Global and Long Term Goals, held at the International Society for Ecological Economics, Washington, D.C., May 1990.

IMF (International Monetary Fund). 1990. *World Economic Outlook*. Washington, D.C., IMF.

MARER, P. 1985. *Dollar GNPs of the USSR and Eastern Europe*. Baltimore, Johns Hopkins University Press.

OECD (Organization for Economic Co-operation and Development). 1990 *a*. *Development Cooperation*. Table 3–1, p. 123. Paris, OECD.

—. 1990*b*. *OECD in Figures*. Paris, OECD.

PRB. 1990 *World Population Data Sheet*.

UNITED STATES DEPARTMENT OF ENERGY. 1988. *Annual Energy Review 1988*. Washington, D.C., United States Department of Energy/Energy Information Agency.

—. 1990. *State Energy Data Report, Consumption Estimates, 1960–1988*. Washington, D.C., United States Department of Energy/Energy Information Agency.

UNITED STATES DEPARTMENT OF COMMERCE. 1975. *Historical Statistics of the United States, Colonial Times to 1970*. (Bicentennial Edition). Washington, D.C., United States Department of Commerce.

VITOUSEK, P. M.; EHRLICH, P.R.; EHRLICH, A.H.; MATSON, P.A. 1986. Human Appropriation of the Products of Photosynthesis. *Bioscience,* Vol. 34, No. 6., pp. 368–73.

WORLD BANK. 1989. *World Debt Tables 1989–1990: External Debt of Developing Countries*. Vols. I and II. Washington, D.C., World Bank.

About the authors

Robert Goodland: Environmental Adviser, Environment Department, World Bank, Washington, D.C. 20433, United States of America. Fax: 202/477–0565. Author of numerous books, mainly on tropical ecology, the most recent being *Race to Save the Tropics* (Island Press, 1990).

Herman Daly: Senior Economist, Environment Department, World Bank, Washington, D.C. 20433, United States of America. Fax: 202/477–0565. Author of many publications on ecological economics including *Steady State Economics* (Freeman, 1974; 2nd edition 1991) and *For the Common Good* with John Cobb, (Beacon Press, 1989).

Trygve Haavelmo and **Stein Hansen**: Respectively, the 1989 Nobel Memorial Prize in Economic Sciences laureat, Institute of Economics, University of Oslo; Director, Nordic Consulting Group A.S. Oslo, Ornev 46A, N–1340 Bekkestua, Norway. Fax: 472/247–856. Stein Hansen is the author of *Economic Policies for Sustainable Development* (Manilla ADB; 1990).

Jan Tinbergen and **Roefie Hueting**: Respectively, the first Nobel Memorial Prize in Economic Sciences laureat and first Chairman of the United Nations Committee on Development Planning; Head, Environmental Statistics, Netherlands Bureau of Statistics. Fax: 31/70/3877–429. Roefie Hueting is the author of *New Scarcity and Economic Growth* (North–Holland Publishing Co. 1980).

Salah El Serafy: Economic Adviser, Economic Advisory Staff, World Bank, Washington, D.C. 20433, United States of America. Fax: 202/477–1569. Author of *Environmental Accounting* (1989).

Bernd von Droste and **Peter Dogsé**: Respectively, Director, Division of Ecological Sciences and Secretary of the Man and the Biosphere Programme; Associate Expert, Division of Ecological Sciences, UNESCO, 7 Place de Fontenoy, 75700 Paris, France. Fax: 331/4065–9897. Authors of *Debt–for–Nature Exchanges and Biosphere Reserves* (UNESCO, 1990).

Robert Costanza: Founding President, International Society for Ecological Economics, P.O. Box 38, Solomons, MD 20688, United States of America. Fax: 301/326–6342. Editor–in–Chief of the journal *Ecological Economics*, and of the 1991 Columbia University text of the same title.

Lester R. Brown, Sandra Postel and **Christopher Flavin**: Respectively, President and Vice–Presidents for Research, Worldwatch Institute, 1776 Massachusetts Avenue NW, Washington, D.C. 20036, United States of America. Fax: 202/296–7365. Worldwatch, a public policy research organization, is devoted to analysing global trends with the aim of promoting a sustainable world economy.